101

school success tools
for students with

ADHD

DATE DUE

101
school success tools
for students with
ADHD

Jacqueline S. Iseman, Ph.D.,
Stephan M. Silverman, Ph.D.,
and Sue Jeweler

PRUFROCK PRESS INC.
WACO, TEXAS

Library of Congress Cataloging-in-Publication Data

Iseman, Jacqueline S., 1977-
101 school success tools for students with ADHD / Jacqueline S. Iseman, Stephan M. Silverman, and Sue Jeweler.
    p. cm.
Includes bibliographical references.
ISBN-13: 978-1-59363-403-2 (pbk.)
ISBN-10: 1-59363-403-X (pbk.)
1. Attention-deficit-disordered children--Education. 2. Attention-deficit hyperactivity disorder--Treatment. I. Silverman, Stephan, 1942- II. Jeweler, Sue, 1947- III. Title. IV. Title: One hundred one school success tools for students with ADHD. V. Title: One hundred and one school success tools for students with ADHD.
    LC4713.2.I84 2010
    371.94--dc22
                    2009050912

Copyright © 2010, Prufrock Press Inc.
Edited by Lacy Compton
Cover and Layout Design by Marjorie Parker

ISBN-13: 978-1-59363-403-2
ISBN-10: 1-59363-403-X

Printed in the United States of America.

At the time of this book's publication, all facts and figures cited are the most current available. All telephone numbers, addresses, and website URLs are accurate and active. All publications, organizations, websites, and other resources exist as described in the book, and all have been verified. The authors and Prufrock Press Inc. make no warranty or guarantee concerning the information and materials given out by organizations or content found at websites, and we are not responsible for any changes that occur after this book's publication. If you find an error, please contact Prufrock Press Inc.

Prufrock Press Inc.
P.O. Box 8813
Waco, TX 76714-8813
Phone: (800) 998-2208
Fax: (800) 240-0333
http://www.prufrock.com

Dedication

In memory of Milton V. Silverman (1917–2009).

In loving memory of Rose Cohen, for always focusing attention on what is genuinely important in life.

To Larry, for his constant attention.

To our wonderful editor, Lacy Compton, for her wise counsel and extraordinary attention to detail.

Contents

List of Tools

Introduction

CHILDREN and adolescents with ADHD often struggle with their day-to-day activities. Inattention can have a profound effect on learning, personal relationships, productivity, personal safety, and self-esteem (Silverman, Iseman, & Jeweler, 2009). The more information we know and understand about ADHD and its impact on individuals, the better able we are to create a thoughtful, collaborative, and effective approach that successfully addresses the strengths and needs of those who deal with their attentional challenges every day.

It is estimated that more than half of children with the primary diagnosis of ADHD have school-related struggles. Specifically, children with ADHD have significantly higher lifetime rates of school dysfunction and lower achievement than their peers. These difficulties include a higher likelihood of grade repetition, need for academic tutoring, or enrollment in a special class. Children with ADHD also are more likely to exhibit impairments in reading and academic achievement as well as higher rates of learning disabilities and school dysfunction (Biederman et al., 1996).

There also appears to be a long-term impact associated with these academic struggles during childhood. Childhood ADHD places individuals at a relative risk for an educational disadvantage throughout life. In adulthood, children diagnosed with ADHD complete less formal schooling than their peers. Although nearly one quarter of children with attention deficits in one study did not complete high school, only 2% of their peers did not complete high school. In addition, while 35% of individuals without ADHD complete a college program, only 5% of students with ADHD complete college (Menhard, 2007).

101 School Success Tools for Students With ADHD provides support materials and the guidance necessary to assist teachers and parents as they empower students to become successful learners. A collection of worksheets, forms, checklists, charts, websites, and other tools are included as reproducible pages.

This book is a companion to *School Success for Kids With ADHD* and contains helpful aids to the teacher and parent as part of a multimodal effort for each child with ADHD. (However, the materials can be used on their own without the companion title.) We strongly believe that the information and tools provided will significantly address the issues faced by individuals with attentional issues. It is important that all of the stakeholders—parents, teachers, other professionals, and the students themselves—work together to create a successful school experience.

The Book Format

The workbook is divided into the following chapters:
✓ Chapter 1: Attention and Planning
✓ Chapter 2: Time Management and Organization
✓ Chapter 3: Homework and Study Skills
✓ Chapter 4: Encouraging Achievement
✓ Chapter 5: Behavior Modification
✓ Chapter 6: Strategies Used by Successful Teachers
✓ Chapter 7: School Observations
✓ Chapter 8: Preparing for Meetings
✓ Chapter 9: Communication Between Teachers, Parents, and Professionals
✓ Chapter 10: Tools for Parents

Each chapter contains the following sections:
✓ introduction,
✓ tips for teacher and/or parent planning and utilization of each tool, and
✓ reproducible tools.

chapter 1

Attention and Planning

NOTHING of value can be accomplished without focus and concentration. The power of concentration characterizes those who truly excel in any field. Achievement requires the ability to sustain attention, to sacrifice other impulses, to resist distraction, to postpone pleasures, and to act with timing and judgment (Silverman et al., 2009).

The problems associated with ADHD are widespread, but especially notable are school performance deficits. It can be overwhelming as a parent or a teacher to know how to help children with ADHD to address difficulties with inattention and planning. In fact, many teachers indicate feeling unprepared to teach children with attention problems and desire more training and strategies to assist them in working more effectively with students with ADHD in the classroom (Silverman et al., 2009). The tools in this chapter will help to address these issues.

Tool 1:
Planning Facilitation

Often children with ADHD have trouble verbalizing their strategies or get stuck using an ineffective strategy repeatedly. Help the student by noting any effective strategies he or she is using, but may not be able to verbalize. Also try to guide the student to develop other strategies if he or she is getting stuck using a strategy that is ineffective or is only effective part of the time.

Tips

Teachers and Parents: Use probes to encourage the child to learn how to plan effectively. The following statements are examples of probes that can be used to encourage children to verbalize their ideas and think about their planning strategies (Naglieri, 1999).

Planning Facilitation

- ✓ How did you do this assignment?
- ✓ What did you notice about the way you completed this assignment?
- ✓ What is a good way to do this assignment?
- ✓ What did this assignment teach you?
- ✓ What seemed to work well for you before?
- ✓ What will you do next time?
- ✓ Can you think of ways to make the assignment easier?
- ✓ Do you think you will do anything differently next time?

Tool 2:
Calming Techniques

The following is a very simple form of meditation, which does not require religious faith, although it may enhance spiritual experience if desired. Although meditation has been demonstrated to provide medical and mental health benefits, the focus of the technique here is calming.

Tips

Teachers and Parents: There are many calming techniques for children including relaxation therapy, yoga, and meditation. The most powerful and simple is meditation.

Calming Techniques

- ✓ Make sure the room is quiet with few distractions.
- ✓ Dim the lights if possible. Ask the children to sit in any position that they can hold for an extended period of time.
- ✓ Each child should feel completely relaxed. There is no need for tension in any part of the body.
- ✓ Ask each child to keep his or her eyes gently closed with the attention focused in the middle of the inside forehead, like a "third eye."
- ✓ Tell the children to repeat any common phrase in the form of a mantra. Examples may include "I believe in myself" or "I am at peace." Continue repeating the calming phrase slowly and in a regular, continuous manner.
- ✓ Soon the nervous system will calm and stabilize. This forms a memory of being calm and can actually help to mitigate primary symptoms of ADHD including inattention, impulsivity, and restlessness and related symptoms such as disorganization and, in many cases, oppositionality.

Tool 3:
Private Speech

Children with ADHD often have difficulty self-monitoring their attention to tasks. Private speech allows these children to quietly self-regulate and keep track of their planning process.

Tips

Teachers and Parents: Teach children to use private speech by first having the child describe his actions aloud and then having the child guide his actions by saying the same thing silently in his head.

Private Speech

Example: To solve the problem $2(4 + 3)^2 - 0(6 \div 2)$, the child could say aloud (and later to herself):

> I need to remember the order of operations.
> It is parentheses, exponents, multiplication and division, addition and subtraction.
> First I need to do everything in parentheses.
> OK, 4 + 3 is 7 and 6 ÷ 2 is 3.
> Now I need to do the exponents.
> OK, 7 squared is 49.
> Next I need to do multiplication.
> OK, 2 times 49 is 98.
> I know that is right because it is the same as 50 times two minus two.
> Hey, wait a minute, 0 times anything is 0.
> So I don't even have to worry about the second half of the equation.
> So the answer is just 98.
> That wasn't so bad!

Tool 4:
Suggested Breaks

Students with ADHD perform better in environments that allow movement and permit the child to get up when necessary. These breaks allow students to refocus and recharge. It typically takes students with ADHD a great amount of effort to focus. Therefore, frequent breaks help in preventing fatigue. Additionally, permitting students to get up and stretch or move during the allotted break will make the students more likely to refocus effectively following the break.

Tips

Teachers and Parents: Individuals with ADHD require frequent breaks to be able to work efficiently. Help students to learn appropriate ways to take breaks according to the situation (in the classroom or in the home).

Suggested Breaks

✓ Getting a drink of water
✓ Stretching
✓ Walking in the hallway
✓ Helping another student or sibling
✓ Helping the teacher or the parent
✓ Drawing or doodling
✓ Running "errands" for the teacher (e.g., getting or giving something to another teacher or the office)
✓ Playing with fidget objects (i.e., squishy toy, dry sponge) during break time

Tool 5:
Self-Monitoring Chart

Teach children to self-monitor by having them rate the progress toward their goals.

Tips

Teachers and Parents: Individuals with ADHD struggle to self-regulate. This chart will help these children learn to self-monitor on-task behavior.

Self-Monitoring Chart

Establish up to five desired behaviors and write them on the chart below. Younger or less developmentally mature children may need to begin with only one goal. At the completion of a specific task or a class period have the student evaluate herself on each of the behaviors with either a "✓" for meeting the goal or an "✗" for not meeting the goal. The teacher or parent should then also evaluate the child with either a "✓" for meeting the goal or an "✗" for not meeting the goal. Award 1 point for each match that the student and adult have so that the student is rewarded for accurately self-monitoring. Also award 1 point for each check that the adult gives so that that student is rewarded for appropriate behavior. Thus a total of 10 points can be earned, up to 5 points for matches and up to 5 points for earning "✓s" from the teacher or parent. Establish a system of rewards based upon points earned (e.g., one minute of computer time for every point earned by the student).

Behavior	Student	Teacher or Parent
1.		
2.		
3.		
4.		
5.		

Tool 6:
Interrupt Passes

This activity rewards children for showing self-control by waiting for a turn to participate in the classroom.

Tips

Teachers: An interrupt pass gives children a fixed number of opportunities to interrupt each day.

Interrupt Passes

In a response-cost design, the child is given a fixed number of opportunities to interrupt each day. The student must hand in a pass after each interruption. At the end of the day the child can collect a prize for every interrupt pass that isn't used. Give the student a fixed number of the passes below to hand to the teacher after each interruption.

Interrupt ★ Pass ★	Interrupt ★ Pass ★
Interrupt ★ Pass ★	Interrupt ★ Pass ★

chapter 2

Time Management and Organization

MANY individuals with ADHD struggle to manage their time effectively and need assistance to develop a better internal sense of time. Frequently, students with ADHD struggle to determine how long it will take to do something or how long it has been between one activity and the next. They often need reminders to complete tasks or timers to help them stay on task until it is time for a break.

Tool 7:
Time Management

Problems with time management are commonplace among individuals with ADHD. This tool assists with these areas of difficulty.

Tips

Teachers and Parents: Keep in mind the limitations of individuals with ADHD. Help students with ADHD to overcome their difficulties with time management by offering supportive and nurturing techniques. Although time management is difficult for a lot of people, remember that it often is particularly difficult for students with ADHD, so try to keep an understanding and accepting attitude.

Time Management

✓ Help students to use timeline charts to break large assignments into smaller pieces, with subdue dates.
✓ Teach students to reward themselves for achieving subdue dates.
✓ Help students learn to use watch devices with reminders, alarms, or buzzers.
✓ Teach students to use planners or computer planning software.
✓ It is important for students to learn to allow enough time for tasks, at first overestimating how long each task or meeting will take, and then becoming better at accurately estimating the time needed to complete tasks (see Tool 8).

Tool 8:
Time Estimation

Students with ADHD often struggle to accurately estimate the amount of time it takes to complete activities. This technique helps these children become more accurate in their predictions of how long it will take to complete a particular task. When children are better able to predict the time it takes to complete tasks, they may become better at time management.

Tips

Teachers and Parents: Have the child write down each of her assignments each day. Help the child prioritize the assignments by giving each a number indicating the order in which she will complete that assignment. Then have the child predict the amount of time she thinks an assignment will take. Set a timer. After the child completes each assignment correctly, have the child record the actual amount of time it took to complete the assignment. Encourage accurate predictions, not quicker completion.

Time Estimation

An example of time estimation for an assignment is provided in the first line of the chart below:

Assignment	Priority	Guess Time	Actual Time
Math, page 113, #1–7	#1	12 minutes	18 minutes

Tool 9:
Organization of Materials

Children with ADHD often have difficulty remembering to bring materials to and from school. It is important to help students learn to be organized from a young age. This checklist makes it possible to help with organization even before the student is reading competently. Help students draw or take photographs of the items that they need to bring to and from school. Help the student put these items on a checklist. (A simply written or typed list can be used once the student is old enough to read competently.) Then teach the student to use this checklist to make sure that all of his or her materials are packed that need to be taken to and from school.

Tips

Teachers and Parents: The list should be made according to the individual needs of the child. The list should be placed in a place where the list needs to be used (e.g., on a desk, in a locker, in a backpack). An example of items to include on the checklist is provided below.

Organizational Checklist

Tool 10: Organizational Technology Checklists

There are many forms of technology on the market that can help with time management. As we continue to learn more about the physiology of ADHD, researchers are able to continuously develop updated technology to address its symptoms. It is essential for parents, teachers, and professionals to keep well informed about the research on technology for helping and treating individuals with ADHD (Silverman et al., 2009).

Tips

Teachers and Parents: Use various forms of technology to help a child organize his or her life. Determine what technology will most directly address the child's area of need.

Organizational Technology Checklists

One type of reminder strategy that often is used by students with ADHD is an alarm clock or a watch that reminds the student throughout the day of his or her responsibilities both at home and at school. One such watch is the WatchMinder, which can be located at http://www.watchminder.com. This watch was developed by a child psychologist to assist children and adults with ADHD to stay focused and manage time effectively.

Use a WatchMinder if:
❏ The child needs a silent alarm/reminder system.
❏ The child needs this reminder with minimal disruption to the child or those nearby.
❏ You want to set up daily routine reminders for the child and want to be able to program up to 30 different activities at a time.
❏ You want to remind and guide particular activities for various types of behavioral modification such as silently encouraging focusing with the message "PAY ATTN."

Timers also are helpful to promote time management. Time Timer (http://www.timetimer.com) is an innovative tool that allows you to see the time elapse by watching the dial that graphically shows how much time is left.

Use Time Timer if:

❏ You want to promote an efficient use of time.

❏ The student needs assistance mastering the concept of time.

❏ You are trying to encourage autonomy and independence.

❏ The student needs assistance with better time management.

❏ The individual needs to keep track of elapsed time in a sound-sensitive environment.

Laptop computers can be used by students with ADHD to aid in written expression without actually writing, to self-edit, and for communication with the school.

Use a laptop computer if:

❏ The student has co-occurring motor difficulties.

❏ The student finds it laborious to write papers by hand.

❏ The child has severe difficulties with legible penmanship.

❏ Parents want to use it for communicating with teachers via e-mail.

❏ The child would benefit from using the computer's spellchecker function or thesaurus, or needs assistance with grammar.

A Personal Digital Assistant (PDA) also can be used to help students with ADHD with time management, keeping track of a schedule, and for reminders.

Use a PDA if:

❏ The student needs a new method to help with keeping track of assignments.

❏ The student needs an alarm or reminder of assignments and activities.

❏ The student needs a timer to keep him on task.

❏ The student has co-occurring motor difficulties or finds it laborious to write down assignments by hand.

Tool 11:
Daily Routine at School

This tool assists teachers in creating a routine for the school day that is clear to students with ADHD.

Tips

Teachers: A daily routine at school is very important in helping establish a feeling of structure and expectations for children with ADHD.

Daily Routine at School

✓ Go over the routine for the next day with your students prior to the end of the school day.

✓ Ask children verbally to repeat tomorrow's plan.

✓ Point to a large calendar on the wall or one in each child's notebook or desk and review the day.

✓ Be sure that all parent permission slips and notices have been supplied for each child's parents for the next day as necessary.

✓ Younger children respond better with frequently repeated visual icons on the calendar.

✓ E-mail the schedule for the next day to each parent who desires it.

✓ Go over the day's schedule each morning by pointing to each planned activity on the calendar.

✓ Be sure that each notification or calendar listing includes what materials will be required.

✓ Tell parents to have their child's backpack containing the next day's required materials, including homework, by the front or back door each evening prior to bedtime.

Tool 12: Task Analysis for Assignments

Effective planning is very important! A task analysis is a way to think about any job. The following is a step-by-step plan that may help students as they break a big assignment into small steps.

Tips

Teachers and Parents: Students with ADHD can benefit greatly from doing a task analysis for their assignments. Teachers should conference with the class or small groups of students after a multistep assignment is given. The steps below can be copied and given to students to help them complete a task analysis.

Task Analysis for Assignments

Step 1: Decide on exactly what you must do.
✓ Find the key words in the directions.
✓ Look carefully at the exact words used.
✓ Say aloud (to yourself) what you must do.
✓ Read the directions one more time.

Step 2: Decide on the number of steps needed to complete the task.
✓ Make a list of all of the steps needed to accomplish the task.
✓ Rank the steps in the order of their importance.

Step 3: Decide on the amount of time each step will take you to do.
✓ Write your steps in the order you ranked them.
✓ Record the amount of time each task will take you to do.

Step 4: Create a schedule.
✓ Count the number of days you have to do the task.
✓ Look at a calendar (see the one on the next page).
✓ Write the day you begin and the deadline date on the calendar.
✓ Plan a time for every step of the task.
✓ Make changes in your time plan when necessary.
✓ Some tasks may take less time.
✓ Some tasks may take more time.

Step 5: Start!
✓ Stay on your schedule.
✓ When you complete a task, record the day you finished the task.
✓ Make changes if needed.
✓ Get help immediately if there is a problem you cannot solve.

Step 6: Finish the task.
✓ Complete it on time—meet the deadline.
✓ Evaluate your finished assignment.
✓ Reward yourself for a job well done!

Calendar

Sunday	Monday	Tuesday	Wednesday	Thursday	Friday	Saturday

Note. Adapted from Montgomery County Public Schools (1983).

Tool 12: Task Analysis for Assignments

Tool 13: Graphic Organizers

Visual tools, known as graphic organizers, most commonly help students to organize their thoughts about something they have read or will be writing about. They also can be used to organize time, review concepts, and plan projects. There are many websites that offer information about the use of graphic organizers with examples that can be pulled off the site for use by teachers (see http://edhelper.com/teachers/graphic_organizers.htm or http://freeology.com/graphicorgs/#).

Tips

Teachers: Graphic organizers are useful tools for students to organize and record information. There are many types of graphic organizers available online and in resource materials. Three of the most commonly used graphic organizers are described below.

Graphic Organizers

A Venn diagram is a graphic organizer that allows students to compare and contrast information. The area of intersection displays the similarities and the outer areas show the differences between topics.

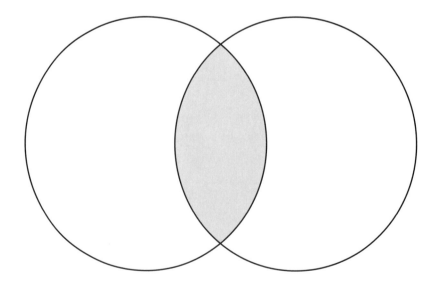

A simple web graphic organizer allows students to record the topic, category, concept, title, or any main idea in the central cell. Based on thinking, research, reading, or any task, the student can record related information in the surrounding cells.

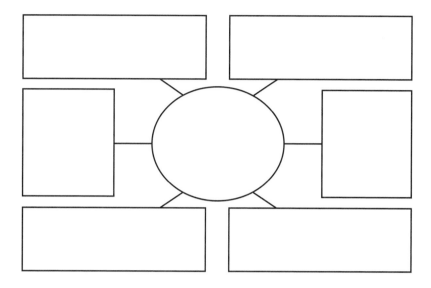

A KWL graphic organizer is used before students begin to explore a topic. The students record what they know (K) and what they want to know (W) about the topic. At the end of the task or assignment, students record what they have learned (L).

Topic:_____

K (What I Know)	W (What I Want to Know)	L (What I Have Learned)

Tool 14:
Smartphones

Many organized and disorganized people of all ages have benefited from electronic handheld information management devices.

Tips

Parents and Teachers: Use the information below to determine if your child or student needs the use of a smartphone to assist him or her in everyday tasks. Some districts may have phones or tablet computers available for student use, but others may require parents to purchase such devices.

Smartphones

Moving beyond personal digital assistants (PDAs), the era of the "smartphone" has arrived with many organizational tools attached as applications on cell phones. Phones, such as Apple's iPhone, are really mini-computers that allow us to communicate by voice, organize information, surf the web, send text messages, share files, and perform almost any other task that full-sized computers are designed to do. Interestingly, the first three versions of the iPhone did not come with a to-do list feature, although this application is now available from third-party application vendors. Applications for the iPhone specifically targeted for people with ADHD are just emerging at this writing.

Tablet PCs also share the advantage with smartphones in utilizing touch-screen ease of use and flexibility. In summer 2009, Apple became engaged in intensive research to develop a tablet-based computer. Tablet PCs have been available from a number of manufacturers using Windows-based software for several years, but are still evolving in their functionality and reliability. The advantage of tablet PCs is their larger keyboards, allowing for faster and less demanding data entry. Like smartphones, tablet PCs will offer greater flexibility in designing personalized access. This is good news for persons with ADHD who will be able to have a to-do list, calendar, contact list, timer alarms, Internet access for information acquisition and exchange, and programmability for ease of use, depending on the nature of their disability or disabilities.

Many parents have reasonable concerns about letting children have these often-expensive devices in their possession. At what age is a child, especially one with ADHD, able to act responsibly with a phone in her possession? Many school systems discourage or do not permit the possession or use of cell phones during the school day or while in class. Many children can be distracted and can be distracting while texting, taking photos, sharing other information, or surfing the net on their phones during instructional time. This factor particularly is a risk for distractible kids with ADHD. Security features such as locks for websites not suitable for children may be nonexistent or of lower functional reliability on handheld devices. The decision to allow a child to possess a smartphone depends on many personal variables in the child's makeup and the parent/child relationship, which are beyond the scope of the authors' ability to make recommendations, because of the individuality of these variables.

Very important caveats to keep in mind in choosing to use a smartphone are the concepts of cognitive load and effortfulness. Applications requiring a lot of sequential steps, the use of working memory, a high level of coordination, extended cognitive effort, and increased complexity make some electronic devices more confusing and frustrating than pencil and paper or mechanical devices. Technology is not always a solution for ADHD.

The following is a list of functions that can be considered as smartphone tools of possible value to persons with ADHD. Keep in mind that ingenious application programmers are developing multiple versions of these tools as we speak:

1. To-do list
2. Timer with alarm
3. Calendar
4. Calculator
5. Contact list
6. Note pad
7. Watch
8. Encyclopedia and dictionary web access
9. Internet search engine (with lockout features)
10. Voice recorder
11. Mapping device

Tool 14: Smartphones

chapter 3

Homework and Study Skills

CHILDREN diagnosed with ADHD often get bored with an activity quickly, particularly if the task is not one that they enjoy. As students, children with ADHD frequently have difficulty remembering to copy down school assignments and to bring home books and other school materials. Additionally, completing homework and studying effectively for tests can be a very large challenge. It is particularly important for students with ADHD to have an appropriate environment in which to complete their homework. The homework setting should be a quiet place in which the child is comfortable and unlikely to be interrupted by external distractions. A routine for completing homework also is important. Children with ADHD benefit from having a consistent time in which they are expected to start working on their homework. Breaks should be permitted periodically, depending upon the child's developmental level and ability to stay focused. Both homework and material on upcoming quizzes and tests should be reviewed with the child.

Tool 15:
Addressing Homework Issues

Many students with ADHD struggle with homework due to their short attention span, restlessness, and impulsivity.

Tips

Parents: Dr. Arthur Robin (n.d.) stressed the importance of collaboration between parents and teenagers to develop an effective homework structure. This structure should be in place throughout much of the student's academic career and should be adjusted to match the degree of independence that the child can handle (Silverman et al., 2009).

Addressing Homework Issues

Robin (n.d.) suggested analyzing the points at which there is a breakdown in the child's or adolescent's homework skills using the following set of questions (*Note*: Although the questions are written for adolescents, they also can be used to identify strengths and weaknesses in children. Additionally, although they are written for parents, teachers also can use them to help address homework issues.)

1. Does your adolescent record the assignments in an assignment book, sheet, planner, or in some other organized manner?
2. Does your adolescent bring home from school the assignment books, textbooks, notebooks, and other materials needed to complete homework?
3. Do you review the assignment book and also have an independent means of ensuring that your adolescent is accurately recording the assignments?
4. Does your adolescent select a quiet, nondistracting, well-lit, and comfortable place in which to do the homework?
5. Do you help your teenager develop an organized plan of attack to sequence multiple homework assignments and study in one evening?
6. Have you and your adolescent agreed upon a starting time for doing homework, and does your adolescent adhere to this agreement?
7. Are you or another responsible adult present in the house to "keep your teenager honest" when you expect him or her to be completing homework?
8. Is your adolescent able to sustain his or her attention long enough to complete the homework? Have breaks been built into the plan?
9. Do you review completed written assignments and quiz your adolescent on material studied for examinations?

10. If your adolescent takes stimulant medication, is there an adequate homework dose "on board" during the designated time?
11. Do you coach your adolescent to use a calendar to track long-term assignments and periodically work on them instead of leaving them for the last minute?
12. Does your adolescent have a plan to make sure that the completed assignments actually get to school and are handed in on time?
13. Are there incentives to motivate your adolescent to do homework? (Robin, n.d., para. 1)

Robin (n.d.) suggested the development of a comprehensive homework plan that addresses the weaknesses that have been identified from the above questions. Then he recommended writing this plan down as a behavioral contract and making sure that the parent and the adolescent sign it. Keep in mind to look for improvement, not perfection. It also is important to have the incentives specifically identified in the contract. Rewards should occur nightly for following the contract (i.e., a specific amount of time on the phone or watching television), as students like immediate gratification, and also can occur weekly (i.e., a sleepover or a trip to the movies) to ensure commitment to long-term goals.

Robin (n.d.) further suggested implementing the contract for several weeks and then revising it as necessary. He recommended that if there are power struggles with the child or teenager or defiance or resistance, a psychologist or other mental health professional be consulted for assistance.

Tool 15: Addressing Homework Issues

Tool 16:
Creating an Appropriate Homework Environment

Individuals with ADHD often are distractible and have difficulty staying on task for even short periods of time. Homework is best completed in areas free of distraction.

Tips

Parents: An environment without distractions that has all of the necessary materials will provide the appropriate structure to increase attention and the likelihood of task completion.

Creating an Appropriate Homework Environment

Create an Organized Work Area
✓ The area should have a table or desk where the child can complete work.
✓ All of the necessary materials should be available in an organized container on or near the work surface.
✓ Other materials that may create a distraction should be removed.

How to Choose a Work Area
✓ An office near where the caregiver will be during the evening provides an area conducive to schoolwork because it has few distractions and is accessible to the caregiver.
✓ Typically the kitchen is too noisy because it often is used for socialization.
✓ The child's bedroom may have distractions and also may be seen as an area of privacy for the child so the caregiver may not have easy access to check on the child.
✓ A phone, TV, or computer in the room is a distraction.

Tool 17:
Strategies for Checking
Over Homework

Students with ADHD sometimes work quickly to complete homework, making frequent errors despite knowing the correct answer.

Tips

Teachers and Parents: Students with ADHD often need assistance paying attention to directions and avoiding carelessness.

Strategies for Checking Over Homework

✓ Encourage children to read the directions aloud before beginning an assignment.
✓ Teach the child to complete the assignment and then check over his work when it is complete.
✓ When you or the child notices that she made a mistake, encourage the child to consider an alternative solution.
✓ Encourage the child to reread the directions when he has completed the assignment and pose the directions as a question or several questions.

> For example, if the directions say: *Complete all of the math problems, and then circle all of the answers with a zero in the tenths place.*

> Have the child ask himself: *Have I completed all of the math problems? Have I circled all of the answers with a zero in the tenths place?*

Tool 18:
Check In–Check Out Technique

Although teens often have developmentally appropriate desires for independence and freedom, teenagers with ADHD still require guidance and help with homework.

Tips

Parents: Use this technique with students to help avoid the power struggle that often occurs around homework.

Check In–Check Out Technique

Check In–Check Out allows students with ADHD to begin to self-monitor their own completion of homework and become more responsible for completing it. Check In–Check Out allows the student to keep track of both short- and long-term assignments and see the week's work at a glance.

At the beginning of the week the student should write down all of the long-term assignments in the top portion of the chart including their due dates. Long-term assignments include any assignments that the student knows about, but are not due the following day. It also includes any quizzes or tests.

In the bottom portion of the chart, the student writes down when he is going to work on each of those long-term assignments including what portion of the assignment he plans to complete those nights. In the bottom portion of the chart the student also should write down any short-term assignments that are due the next day. Next to each short- and long-term assignment the student should make a box that will later be checked when the assignment is complete.

Once all of the short- and long-term assignments have been written down, the student should "check in" with a parent to show the plan for the week and for the night. The specific time that evening that the "check out" will occur should be decided. Then the student completes the work, checking off each assignment as it is completed and the student comes to the parent for the check out. If all of the work is complete, the check out is finished. Throughout the week, the student should continue to add all short- and long-term assignments as they are received.

To begin, teach the student how to use the Check In–Check Out strategy by showing him how it is used. Once the student is comfortable with the technique, allow him to complete his homework independently (aside from checking in and checking out)

Long-Term Assignments and Due Dates

1.

2.

3.

4.

5.

Schedule for Short-Term and Long-Term Assignments

Monday	Tuesday	Wednesday	Thursday	Friday

Tool 18: Check In–Check Out Technique

Tool 19:
Using Technology
for Homework

Technology is important because it can open new opportunities for accessing education and can help break down the barriers to learning for children and adolescents with ADHD (Silverman et al., 2009).

Tips

Teachers and Parents: Technology changes exponentially over time. Therefore, it is imperative that professionals, parents, and other people involved in the lives of individuals with ADHD keep abreast of the new technology and how it can be used to support people with ADHD (Silverman et al., 2009).

Using Technology for Homework

Throughout the last several decades, rapid growth in the area of technology has impacted our lives. Similarly, over the years there has been a significant increase in the types of technological options available for assisting individuals with ADHD with their homework.

Kurzweil 3000

Kurzweil Educational Systems (2006; see http://www.kurzweiledu.com) has developed research-based technologies that are intended to help students in elementary school through college with learning challenges succeed academically. The Kurzweil assistive technology programs target reading, writing, and study solutions. The website states that the use of assistive technology such as Kurzweil 3000 is an important accommodation for struggling students. Without such accommodations, the Kurzweil Education Systems website stated that it is sometimes nearly impossible for struggling readers to catch back up academically. In a study of how assistive reading software impacted the reading performance of students with attention disorders (Hecker, Burns, Katz, Elkind, & Elkind, 2002), the students used this assistive technology software for the majority of a semester in order to read assignments for an English class. The Kurzweil 3000 program provided students a synchronized visual and auditory presentation of the book and incorporated study skills tools for learning how to highlight and take notes effectively. The results suggested that the assistive software permitted the students to pay better attention during the reading, to reduce their distractibility, to read with decreased stress and fatigue, and to be able to read for a longer duration. The program helped the students with attention disorders to read faster, completing reading assignments in a shorter period of time. Although it did not have a large impact on comprehension for all students, it helped some students who had comprehension that was very poor. According to Hecker et al. (2002), assistive reading software should be considered as an effective intervention and as an accommodation that will assist students who have attention disorders and a problem with sustained effort to help compensate for their disorders. The purpose of the Kurzweil system initially was to help people with significant reading decoding problems by providing immediate text-to-speech context, but the technology may facilitate better attention to text, too, by doing some of the decoding work that might labor attention systems and working memory.

Inspiration Software

Inspiration Software Inc. (see http://www.inspiration.com) developed Kidspiration for kindergarteners through fifth graders and Inspiration for students in grades 6–12. These tools help students to learn to plan, research, and complete projects effectively using graphic organizers that expand simple topics into more detailed writing.

The version for younger children, Kidspiration, provides students with a simple way to use research-based visual learning principles to build graphic organizers by combining pictures, text, and spoken words in order to represent the student's thoughts and information. Kidspiration intends to develop students' achievement by promoting the following skills:

✓ categorizing and grouping,
✓ developing emerging literacy skills,
✓ building comprehension skills, and
✓ expressing and organizing thoughts.

Inspiration, the version for middle school and high school students, is similar as it also relies on visual learning. Students create their own graphic organizers to represent their own ideas and relationships and then use the integrated outlining function to further organize ideas for writing. This program assists older students in improving their critical thinking, comprehension, and writing skills across a variety of subjects. Inspiration is intended to improve skills in the areas of:

✓ analyzing complex topics,
✓ improving writing proficiency, and
✓ developing planning skills.

Tool 19: Using Technology for Homework

The possible benefit of Inspiration software is to provide a skeleton in order to facilitate executive function through guided planning.

Alternatives to Printed Text

Some students with ADHD also may require or benefit from other mediums than standard printed books, such as books on tape. A federally funded national repository known as the National Instructional Materials Access Center (NIMAC) has digital versions of textbooks and other instructional materials that can be easily converted into accessible formats. Created under the Individuals with Disabilities Education Improvement Act of 2004, the NIMAC attains digitally formatted books from textbook publishers, and then allows authorized users within the United States to download the material through an online database. Once the download is complete, these files can be used to produce various specialized formats, including Braille, audio, or digital text for elementary or secondary school students that qualify. Books on tape provide a similar benefit as Kurzweil in lifting the burden of attention on decoding and working memory. In addition, Recording for the Blind and Dyslexic (http://www.rfbd.org) offers services to parents, students, teachers, and educational professionals (Silverman et al., 2009). Both Windows and Mac computers also can offer support in reading text aloud to students.

Tool 20:
Skills for Using a Textbook

Students with ADHD often benefit from learning the most effective way to access information from a textbook.

Tips

Teachers and Parents: Use this guide to help kids with ADHD use textbooks in and out of class. Teachers may want to turn this list into a chart or poster to display in the classroom.

Skills for Using a Textbook

Here are some quick tips for studying from a textbook:

Have a purpose for reading.
✓ What do you need to learn?
✓ Why do you need to learn it?
✓ Where will you find the information you need?

Use good strategies.
✓ List the things you want to know.
✓ Check out the Table of Contents.
✓ Check out the topic headings in boldface print.
✓ Take notes.
✓ Review your notes.

Survey the chapter.
✓ Read the first two paragraphs.
✓ Read the boldface subtopics and headings.
✓ Read the last two paragraphs.
✓ Look at the graphics, pictures, diagrams, and maps.
✓ Read the captions for the graphics.
✓ Now go back to the beginning and read the chapter.

chapter 4

Encouraging Achievement

T H E goal of every life is crowned by self-knowledge and the self-realization of strengths. When these realized strengths are combined with passion and a personal mission, then the power of attention can be focused and enabled. It is our hope that every child, especially those with challenges in attending and restraining action, can be recognized for his or her strengths and that the power of self-knowledge and passion can be harnessed and focused for his own fulfillment (Silverman et al., 2009). The following practices can help encourage achievement.

Provide Strength-Based Instruction to Encourage Achievement

Sammy, one of Ms. Smith's students, is diagnosed with ADHD. After reviewing all of the school information regarding Sammy, she began to analyze the implications for instruction. Through an Interest Survey, a student conference, informal and formal diagnostic testing, careful observation, staff input, parent input, and contact with Sammy's pediatrician and psychologist, Ms. Smith was able to carefully plan appropriate instruction. She recognized Sammy's strengths, interests, talents, learning style, and his needs regarding attentional issues (Ricci, Barnes-Robinson, & Jeweler, 2006).

Sammy is a bright child who is strong in the visual-spatial area and is a visual and hands-on learner. Ms. Smith learned that Sammy has a good long-term visual memory, sees relationships, thinks primarily in pictures, learns complex concepts eas-

ily, is creative and intuitive, has a sophisticated sense of humor, is good at math reasoning, and loves to build and construct with a variety of materials.

Sammy's attention issues result in the following: having a lack of attention to detail on written work, missing important verbal and nonverbal cues, doing poor planning for assignments, making many careless errors, and missing deadlines.

Research and a review of successful programs indicate that the most important component of the education of these students is providing instruction in the student's area of strength. Working through a child's strengths puts a positive spin on learning, especially for a student who has had continued difficulty in school (Weinfeld, Barnes-Robinson, Jeweler, & Roffman Shevitz, 2006). In addition, encouraging a student's strengths builds self-confidence in her ability to learn material. For example, an assignment that asks a student to build a web page on the daily lives of soldiers in the Civil War in lieu of a traditional report could connect a student's strength in technology with new material being taught in the classroom, in this case, an aspect of the Civil War. Teachers also can implement a student's strengths in a particular area by allowing her to serve as an expert on the topic or method. Some students delight in being given new responsibilities connected to their strengths, especially if they previously were given instruction that only addressed their weaknesses. Such emphasis on strengths can be accomplished by differentiating instruction, a classroom tool recommended for use with all students and described in the next section (Silverman et al., 2009).

Students may benefit from exploring how well-known, smart people overcame their own difficulties. Some of the following tools help to give students insight into how those who struggled with learning became successful people who made lasting contributions to society. Their stories become springboards for encouraging student achievement.

Tool 21:
Strength-Based Instruction

Working through a child's strengths puts a positive spin on learning, especially for a student who has had continued difficulty in school. Instruction, when it is differentiated, better matches an individual's abilities, styles, and needs.

Tips

Teachers: Use this tool as a self-evaluation checklist. Use this tool when planning for instruction and to communicate with parents, other staff members, and students.

Strength-Based Instruction Checklist

- ❏ Study and practice models for education (e.g., Bloom's Taxonomy)
- ❏ Provide activities that focus on students' individual gifts and interests
- ❏ Provide open-ended outlets for the demonstration of knowledge
- ❏ Use differentiated instruction
- ❏ Provide tasks that fit students' learning styles
- ❏ Provide multisensory instruction
- ❏ Provide guided discovery, especially when introducing new topics
- ❏ Give students choices
- ❏ Use collaboratively designed rubrics
- ❏ Provide hands-on experiences
- ❏ Provide real-life tasks
- ❏ Integrate visual and performing arts

Content
- ❏ Use multiple texts
- ❏ Use varied resources
- ❏ Compact curriculum
- ❏ Provide learning contracts

Process
- ❏ Use interactive journals
- ❏ Use tiered assignments
- ❏ Create interest centers
- ❏ Create learning centers

Product

❏ Provide varied modes of expression, materials, and technologies
❏ Require advanced assignments that require higher order thinking skills
❏ Provide authentic assessment
❏ Use self- and peer evaluations

Note. Adapted from Weinfeld et al. (2006).

Tool 22:
They Did It! So Can I!:
Famous People With Learning
Difficulties or ADHD

Some well-known individuals provide the inspiration for kids, their parents, and their teachers to imagine that they too can achieve great things. It helps to understand that others who we look to as successful role models also experienced learning difficulties.

Tips

Teachers: Use with the whole class, small groups, or individuals. You can integrate this type of activity into the curriculum. For example, if a character in a literary piece has learning challenges, this activity will give insight to students. Help students recognize that kids with challenges have great potential for success.

They Did It! So Can I!: Famous People With Learning Difficulties or ADHD

Hans Christian Andersen
Alexander Graham Bell
Orlando Bloom
James Carville
Winston Churchill
Bill Cosby
Tom Cruise
Patrick Dempsey
Leonardo Da Vinci
Walt Disney
Albert Einstein
Malcolm Forbes
Henry Ford
Benjamin Franklin
Galileo
Danny Glover
Whoopi Goldberg

Salma Hayek
Tommy Hilfiger
Bruce Jenner
Jewel
Magic Johnson
Keira Knightley
John Lennon
Jay Leno
Carl Lewis
Greg Louganis
Sir Isaac Newton
Michael Phelps
Keanu Reeves
Pete Rose
Babe Ruth
Nolan Ryan
Charles Schwab
Steven Spielberg
Quentin Tarantino
Henry Winkler
Robin Williams
Woodrow Wilson
Frank Lloyd Wright
and the list goes on . . .

Directions:

✓ Choose a person from the list above or from another source.
✓ Research information about the person.
✓ Once you have collected information, create a product that informs an audience about the individual you have studied. You may:
  - write a report,
  - make a storyboard,
  - design an exhibit,
  - make a scrapbook,
  - record information,
  - create a video,
  - perform a skit,
  - create a collage,
  - write a poem, or
  - design your own product.

Note. Adapted from Weinfeld et al. (2006).

Tool 23:
Stories of Struggles
That Led to Success

Some people with ADHD have gone on to have very successful careers in various areas. However, even these people struggled with their ADHD in childhood, as a teen, and even in young adulthood.

Tips

Teachers: Like the aforementioned technique, this lesson can be used with the whole class, small groups, or individuals. Teachers can integrate this lesson into research units or curriculum regarding character studies, historical periods, or citizenship.

Stories of Struggles That Led to Success

Howie Mandel—Comedian and Actor: "When I was in high school, my impulsivity led me to all kinds of acts and pranks. I had trouble sitting still and could hardly focus or pay attention in class. It was probably due to my AD/HD that my high school days were filled with impulsive actions and pranks such as calling contractors from the Yellow Pages at lunch to get a bid on an addition to our school library. The principal noticed my scheme when he saw contractors measuring the school grounds. When he went outside to see what was going on, the contractors told him they were there to measure the area to place a bid for the addition. Dumbfounded, the principal asked who authorized this, and they said 'Howie Mandel!'" (Matlen, 2008, para. 4)

Frank Winfield Woolworth—(1852–1919)—Department Store Innovator: Founded a retail company that was one of the original American five-and-dime stores and grew it to be one of the largest retail chains in the world through most of the 20th century. However, earlier in his career, while he was working in a dry goods store at 21 years old, his employers would not even let him wait on a customer because he "didn't have enough sense."

Albert Einstein—(1879–1955)—Physicist: Einstein is most well known for developing the theories of special relativity and general relativity. He received the Nobel Prize in Physics in 1921. However, lore suggests that Einstein was 4 years old before he could speak, and 7 before he could read.

Thomas Edison—(1847–1931)—Inventor: Edison was a famous American inventor, scientist, and businessman. He developed a number of devices that significantly influenced everyday life around the world. These inventions included the phonograph, the motion picture camera, and the first long-lasting, practical electric light bulb. However, when he was younger his teachers told him he was too stupid to learn anything.

Walt Disney—(1901–1966)—Founded the Walt Disney Company: Walt Disney was a film producer and a popular American showman. He was well known as an innovator in animation and theme park design. Along with his staff he created a number of the world's most famous cartoon characters including Mickey Mouse. He also received 59 Academy Award nominations. In addition, he won 26 Oscars, including a record four in one year, and seven Emmy Awards. Disneyland and Walt Disney World Resort theme parks in the United States, Japan, France, and China are all named after him. However, earlier in his career, a newspaper editor fired him because he had "no good ideas."

Louis Pasteur—(1822–1895)—Scientist: Pasteur was a French chemist and microbiologist. He is most well known for his breakthroughs in the causes and methods to prevent disease. He was best known for inventing a method to stop milk and wine from causing sickness to humans, and the process that came to be called pasteurization was named after him. However, when he attended the Royal College he was rated as mediocre in chemistry.

Wernher von Braun—(1912–1977)—Rocket Scientist: He was a rocket physicist and astronautics engineer and became one of the leading figures in developing rocket technology within Germany and the United States. In fact, he is sometimes said to be the preeminent rocket engineer of the 20th century. However, when he was in ninth grade he flunked algebra.

Tool 24:
Catch a Student Being Good

It is important to try to reinforce appropriate behavior. When teachers and parents focus on inappropriate behaviors, students often are encouraged to display more negative behavior to continue receiving attention. Instead try to catch children doing something appropriate and help students recognize appropriate behavior and feel good about it. When a child feels encouraged, he or she will be more likely to repeat the positive behavior.

Tips

Teachers and Parents: Develop a reward system focused around catching students being good. Some teachers and parents use poker chips or tickets with smiley faces on them. Children can earn one chip or ticket every time they do something appropriate. Come up with a system where the children can earn prizes or rewards. For example, for every five chips or tickets the child earns, the child gets a sticker to put on the chart below. When the child earns 20 stickers, he or she can earn a larger prize at school such free time, computer time, or a homework pass. At home rewards such as special trips/activities, the choice of where to eat dinner, or a sleepover can be used.

Catch a Student Being Good

Student's Name _____

Reward for 20 Stickers _____

Tool 25:
Verbal Encouragement

Children with ADHD tend to have low self-esteem. Thus, it is even more important to verbally encourage these children in order to reinforce on-task behavior.

Tips

Teachers and Parents: It is important to have the perspective of encouraging appropriate and desired behaviors rather than just punishing inappropriate behaviors.

Verbal Encouragement

A positive, hopeful, optimistic, and cheerful attitude should be a natural component of teachers' and parents' verbal repertoire, because all children can learn and improve. Praise does not go to the child's head when honestly earned. Children can detect when praise is unwarranted or not genuine. Praise is a very powerful motivator. When it is given continuously without discrimination however, it is less powerful in sustaining good habits than when it is periodic and truly earned.

The *CHADD Information and Resource Guide to AD/HD* (Children and Adults with Attention-Deficit/Hyperactivity Disorder; Harman, 2001) specifically recommended using words of encouragement that increase the child's feeling of acceptance.

Examples of such statements include:
✓ "I like the way you tackled that problem."
✓ "I'm glad you're pleased about your work."
✓ "How do you feel about it?"
✓ "I hadn't though about that idea. Good thinking."

Parents can increase their child's confidence by using statements such as:
✓ "That's rough. I know you can get it."
✓ "You'll figure it out."
✓ "I have confidence that you'll solve it."
✓ "You're right on track. Keep thinking of those good ideas."

It also is important to emphasize the child's contributions:
✓ "I really appreciate your effort in math today."

✓ "You've become the best speller in the family."

✓ "Your hard work really helped a lot."

Finally, it is important to recognize the child's effort and improvement including:

✓ "You really made good effort on that."

✓ "I can see the result of your effort. It looks great!

✓ "Look at the progress you've made."

✓ "Your practice is really paying off."

Tool 26:
The Animal School Fable

This story and its discussion questions allow children to think about the learning process.

Tips

Teachers: Read the fable to the class. Discuss its meaning using the questions following the fable. Give the fable to parents at conference time or use it in training sessions with parents or other teachers.

The Animal School Fable

Once upon a time, the animals decided they must do something to prepare their young to face the challenges of the world, and so they organized a school. They adopted an activity curriculum consisting of running, climbing, swimming, and flying, and to make sure all animals were competent in all of the important skills, all of the animals had to take all of the subjects.

The Duck was an excellent swimmer, better in fact than his instructor, and made passing grades in flying, but he was very poor in running. Because he was slow in running, he had to stay after school and also spend less time swimming in order to spend more time practicing his running. This was continued until his webbed feet were badly worn, and he was only average in swimming. But, average was acceptable in the new animal school, so nobody worried about that except the Duck.

The Rabbit started at the top of his class in running, but he had a nervous breakdown because of so much make-up work in swimming.

The Squirrel was excellent in climbing until he developed frustration in the flying class where his teacher made him start from the ground up instead of from the treetop down. His feelings of frustration spilled over to his other classes and he ended up with a C in climbing and a D in running.

The newest student in the school was an abnormal animal called the Snakehead Fish. At the end of the year the snakehead, which could swim very well and also climb out of the water and walk on the land, was the valedictorian of the school.

Guided Questions for Discussion

1. Which animal do you resemble? Why?
2. Why were the animals unsuccessful?
3. Why was the Snakehead Fish valedictorian?
4. What is the "moral" of this fable?
5. How is this school similar to and different from your school experience?
6. What would you suggest as a different plan for the school in the fable?
7. Did you find this fable amusing? Why or why not?

Note. Adapted from Weinfeld et al. (2006).

chapter 5

Behavior Modification

CHILDREN and adolescents with ADHD often struggle with their day-to-day activities. Inattention can have a profound effect on learning, personal relationships, productivity, personal safety, and self-esteem (Silverman et al., 2009).

A behavioral plan is not a cure for ADHD. However, it can be extremely helpful. Teachers and parents find that a student's behavior is more appropriate while the plan is being implemented, but the unwanted behaviors return once it is discontinued. If assistance is needed in creating a more permanent system of changes to the child's behavior, it often is beneficial to consult with a psychologist or other qualified mental health professional. Receiving parent permission to keep in contact with professionals outside of the schoolhouse is a partnership that supports the student.

Tips for behavior management include:
✓ Develop good rapport with your students.
✓ Implement a plan or develop an functional behavioral analysis and behavioral intervention plan with the school team.
✓ Reinforce positive behavior.
✓ Selectively ignore inappropriate behavior.
✓ Develop a token or reward system.
✓ Assign responsibilities that require self-control.

Tips for classroom management include:
✓ Post rules in the classroom.

✓ Post routines and schedules in the classroom.
✓ Give verbal and visual cues and prompts.
✓ Simplify directions and repeat them clearly.

Tool 27:
Goal Development

These questions should guide discussions with students to establish and then monitor progress on their goals.

Tips

Teachers and Parents: It is important to help children develop both short- and long-term goals. Short-term goals include the steps that help students to reach a long-term goal.

Goal Development

Heacox (1991) created a list of questions used to identify both short- and long-term goals.

✓ What is one area of my school or life performance I want to improve?
✓ What is one thing I can do to accomplish my long-term goal?
✓ How can this goal be broken down into a step-by-step plan?
✓ What is good about doing this? What are the benefits to me?
✓ What are the things that might get in my way as I work toward my goal?
✓ What special materials or help will I need to reach my goal?
✓ How will I reward myself when I achieve my goal?
✓ How will I check on my progress and make sure that my plan is working?
✓ How will I remind myself of my goal?
✓ How is my plan working? Is it working well? If not, why not?
✓ Does my plan need to be revised?
✓ Is the goal still necessary, important, and appropriate?
✓ Is the incentive right?
✓ Have I reached my goal?

Tool 28:
Behavioral Contract

Children with ADHD function best in a system in which there are clear and frequently reviewed expectations.

Tips

Teachers: The contract should be developed in collaboration with the child. Incorporate a clear reward system whereby the child can gain privileges or rewards for accomplishing small goals.

Behavioral Contract

This is a contract between _____ and _____.
(child's name)　　　　　　　　　　　　*(teacher's name)*

The contract starts on _____ and ends on _____.
(start date)　　　　　　　　　　*(end date)*

During the school day, we agree to _____ the behavior of
(increase or decrease)

_____. The contract ends when the behavior is
(specific target or problematic behavior)

_____ to _____.
(increased or decreased)　　*(frequency or number of times per week or day)*

At that time _____ will earn _____.
(child's name)　　　　　　　　　*(specific privilege or reward)*

Teacher's signature _____

Child's signature _____

Tool 29:
Five Finger Method of
Behavioral Modification

Younger children with ADHD often benefit from a visual system of cueing and tracking self-control.

Tips

Teachers and Parents: Develop five appropriate, positively worded goals for the child (i.e., keep hands and feet to self, follow directions, raise hand to be called on). Trace the child's hand. Write one goal on each finger. Track the child's behaviors at specific intervals throughout the day. Allow the child to earn predetermined rewards based on the number of points earned.

Five Finger Method of Behavioral Modification

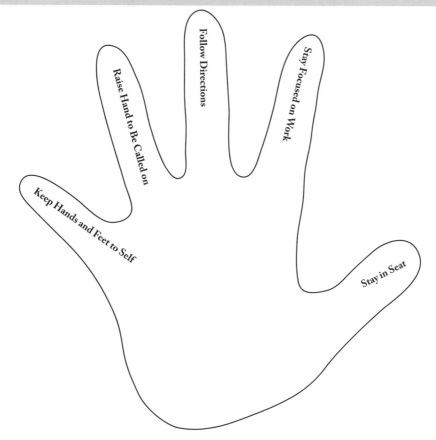

Tool 30:
Behavioral Interventions
Checklist

Set up the environment to ensure that students can be successful, using the following checklist as a guide.

Tips

Teachers: Kids do well when they can do well. Keeping this philosophy in mind is important to ensure that the classroom is structured to create a successful environment.

❏ Set up highly structured routines and realistic, consistent expectations.
❏ Anticipate problem situations and teach skills that children lack—Be proactive!
❏ Use immediate consequences (e.g., praise, rewards, and privileges) for task completion.
❏ Use a greater frequency of positive consequences than discipline (use a system of earning privileges).
❏ Give feedback on how behaviors affect others.
❏ Write out, post, and hand out student responsibilities early in the year and refer to them whenever necessary.
❏ Make sure rules are consistent throughout school (e.g., all classrooms, hallways, lunchroom, recess, gym, and bus).
❏ Every student should be trained beginning the first day of school about expectations for behavior related to safety, responsibility, respect, and relationships.
❏ Students should be rewarded for displaying appropriate behavior (i.e., catch students behaving appropriately).

Tool 31:
STOP Method:
Stop, Think, Options, Plan

Children with ADHD often need reminders to use an organized method of problem solving rather than acting on impulse.

Tips

Teachers and Parents: Teach children to use the STOP method of problem solving, then encourage children to use it independently.

STOP Method: Stop, Think, Options, Plan

Stop: Stop what you are doing. Don't act!

Think: Put on your thinking cap. Don't make impulsive decisions based on your feelings at that moment.

Options: Think of three different options and consider the advantages and disadvantages of each.

Plan: Thoughtfully choose a plan with the most advantages and least disadvantages.

chapter 6

Strategies Used by Successful Teachers

SUCCESSFUL teachers find ways to unleash the potential and free the power within their students. They provide strategies that circumvent student deficits and create an environment that promotes student self-efficacy and self-sufficiency. Children with ADHD rarely find themselves actively engaged in instruction to the same degree as children without the disorder. Their access to instruction needs to be facilitated by specific instructional strategies. The following strategies assist students in completing tasks and assignments and empower students to demonstrate their knowledge and understanding of concepts and content.

Learn, Teach, Practice, and Model Strategies That Support and Empower Students Who Have Difficulties Related to ADHD

Ms. Smith reads the prominent research and literature suggested by her counselor and school psychologist, attends school in-services, speaks with her professional colleagues, talks to her students' doctors, and uses the resources and materials available regarding children with learning difficulties. She individualizes instruction and chooses the appropriate strategies for her children. She learns, teaches, practices, and models the best practices.

It is of the utmost importance that teachers keep abreast of the advancements in current research related to this student population so that the activities and materials used in the classroom are the most effective. The following list of categories and strategies can be helpful as a structure for the educator's storehouse of information (Dendy, 2006; DuPaul & Eckert, 1998; McIntyre, 2004; U.S. Department of Education, 2004):

✓ The classroom environment should be/have:
- mutually respectful,
- accepting,
- exciting,
- flexible,
- organized materials,
- additional classroom supplies available,
- student placement away from distractions,
- permission for student to move freely,
- student choices, and
- positive reinforcement.

✓ Academics should include:
- strength-based instruction,
- differentiation,
- modified pace,
- alternative products,
- ongoing evaluation, and
- peer tutoring.

✓ Adaptations/Accommodations (IEP/504 Plan) should include:
- extended time;
- task modification;
- breaking tasks into segments;
- frequent breaks;
- strategy training;
- interim deadlines;
- highlighting of key points, words, and directions;
- preferential seating;
- student assignment sheet/pad/notebook;
- allowance for "fidget toys"; and
- additional textbooks for home.

✓ Social/Emotional strategies include:
- positive reinforcement,
- promotion of student awareness,

- use of contracts, and
- teaching of social skills.

In addition, many resources for teachers detail appropriate adaptations and accommodations that target students' disabilities, allowing them to understand and present mastery of the material in a manner appropriate to their strengths. Teachers may utilize the Internet to explore appropriate sites and also tap the expertise of those within the school and school system. An eclectic collection of "what works" is necessary for a teacher to have in order to meet the specific needs of students with ADHD. Once the teacher has acquired information, she can then plan and model the best practices (Silverman et al., 2009).

Create an Environment of Mutual Respect, Acceptance, Organization, Flexibility, and High Expectations

As each student entered Ms. Smith's classroom, she greeted him or her with a smile and a few words. As the result of a full group discussion, classroom rules and standards were created and clearly posted on the board and one of the many colorful information stations on the walls. These rules reflected the academic, behavior, and social goals agreed upon by the class. Ms. Smith explained the organization of her classroom including the typical schedule, the routines, the open lines of communication, and her expectations for a successful year. At the beginning of the school year, Ms. Smith set the climate for collaboration, caring, respect, and negotiation for the year.

Good classrooms become a place where risk-taking is encouraged and making mistakes is the way one grows and learns. The environment in such classrooms is not competitive, but rather a place where students measure their progress internally and receive a sense of worth and accomplishment from within. Student strengths are recognized and rewarded early and regularly. The teacher models a sense of unconditional acceptance and responsibility.

Classroom rules should be established by the students, with adult guidance, in a spirit of fairness and an appreciation and valuing of individual differences. The rules should be posted in a prominent place and always referred to when problems arise. Problem-solving processes need to be formally taught and practiced throughout the year, and students should be expected to apply them as needed. Students should use these skills in their relationships in school, as well as be able to recognize when these skills are used in literature, history, and social studies. These skills have real-world applications and consequences. The problem-solving processes are posted in prominent places for easy reference. Many classrooms have a suggestion box where students are encouraged to share ideas to improve the sense of community in the classroom.

Classroom organization must be flexible, yet structured, with opportunities for collaborative goal setting, significant peer interactions, and cooperative learning. Students should be immersed in a climate that promotes self-efficacy and a solid sense of self-sufficiency while being provided with instruction that demands the use of their abilities. By maintaining high expectations and standards in an atmosphere of support, humor, and comfort, teachers help students grow academically and love learning (Silverman et al., 2009; Weinfeld et al., 2006).

Differentiate Instruction

Ms. Smith, working with Sammy's case manager and using his IEP, gives Sammy preferential seating, uses manipulatives in math, and incorporates visual aids like graphic organizers and diagrams with Sammy. She gives him highlighters to focus on key words and ideas and provides hands-on activities that capture his attention. She provides a color-coded assignment book to write down all of his assignments that they will check each day in order to address his attention issues. She provides opportunities for classroom computer access and assistive technology whenever needed. Ms. Smith, recognizing his visual-spatial skills and interests, allows him to do alternative products that reflect his clear understanding of concepts and content material.

Instruction, when it is differentiated, better matches an individual's abilities, styles, and needs. Differentiation is a way of thinking and planning in order to meet the diverse needs of students based on their characteristics. Teachers differentiate content, process, and product according to students' readiness, interest, and learning profiles through a range of instructional and management strategies (Renzulli, 1977; Tomlinson, 1999).

Content is the subject matter prescribed by the state or district program of studies. For example, in social studies, students may be asked to write a research paper on the Civil War. *Process* is the internalization of information. Following the steps for the paper from notes, outline, and draft stages illustrates a process a student follows when dealing with the content material. Some children with ADHD may need to break the tasks into smaller parts and have check-in points with the teacher. *Product* is the outcome of the application of the processes to the content. The finished research paper is the product. Providing differentiation for these students, a variety of resources could be used to study the Civil War (content); organizational software and assisted note-taking may aid in internalizing information (process); and the student may demonstrate his understanding through a model, dramatization, or PowerPoint presentation (product; Weinfeld et al., 2006).

The following are examples of specific ways to differentiate instruction in each of the three categories (Tomlinson, 1999):

Content
- ✓ Use multiple texts
- ✓ Use varied resources
- ✓ Compact curriculum
- ✓ Provide learning contracts

Process
- ✓ Use interactive journals
- ✓ Use tiered assignments
- ✓ Create interest centers
- ✓ Create learning centers

Product
- ✓ Provide varied modes of expression, materials, and technologies
- ✓ Require advanced assignments that require higher order thinking skills
- ✓ Provide authentic assessment
- ✓ Use self- and peer evaluations

Provide Appropriate Interventions, Adaptations, and Accommodations

Ms. Smith meets with Sammy and his parents to discuss his IEP goals and the adaptations and accommodations he will be receiving in class. They discuss Sammy's strengths and needs. His counselor, the school psychologist, and a special education resource teacher might choose to attend this meeting. A case manager on the team will be established—Ms. Smith or a school special education teacher in this case—and a regular channel of communication will be established (his parents prefer to communicate with his case manager and school staff via an office e-mail address). They agree on specific days of the week and best times in case a voice conference is required.

They work out the signals that will act as cues to Sammy to listen to directions. In addition, they plan on ways to help Sammy pay attention to details in his written work. A task analysis and calendar are set up for each major assignment. In order to tap into Sammy's interest in building, a mentor, who is an architect, has been contacted to work with Sammy on a one-on-one project. Sammy will join a "lunch bunch" with the school counselor to reinforce strategies that address his attentional issues.

Evaluation is an important component when providing appropriate adaptations and accommodations. Ms. Smith sets up conferences with Sammy about progress on his goals. A daily assignment sheet is signed by the teacher for accuracy, sent home with Sammy each day, and is returned the next day with a parent signature. He and his parents will agree to the plan, and a system of rewards will be established at home for positive behavior and progress on his goals at school. Ms. Smith is diligent about positive reinforcement and support.

As Sammy shows improvement, a goal may be adjusted or dropped. However, Ms. Smith recognizes that ongoing evaluation is essential.

When it is suspected that a student has ADHD, it is crucial that the adults who are involved come together with the student to analyze the student's strengths and needs and then together create an appropriate intervention plan. Creating this plan calls for analyzing a student's strengths, as well as his or her challenges. Next, the current program is evaluated to see how well it is nurturing and developing the student's strengths, on one hand, while adapting and accommodating for his weaknesses on the other. Finally, recommendations are made for program changes that will result in the appropriate level of challenge, and the instruction and support that will develop the student's strengths and strengthen his or her weaknesses. Psychological and educational testing may be required in some cases to identify strengths and needs. (For more information see pp. 242–251 of *School Success for Kids With ADHD*.)

Once a student's strengths and challenges have been explored, take a close look at the current program to see how well it is addressing both the identified strengths and challenges. Examine what rigorous programming is already in place to address the student's strengths. Next, explore the variety of supports, interventions, and instruction that are in place to both circumvent weaknesses and provide opportunities for strengthening them. Analyze the adaptations and accommodations that are currently in place. Look at the special instruction in which the student is participating in order to strengthen the weaknesses. Look at the special behavior management plans and counseling that are in place to meet the student's behavioral needs. Finally, look at the case management practices to ensure that all pieces are being addressed appropriately and that there is effective communication between and among all staff and parents.

After completing a thorough analysis of the student's strengths and weaknesses and the current instruction and interventions that are in place, make recommendations about adjustments in the student's program. These recommendations become the intervention plan that helps each student reach his or her potential. The intervention plan includes recommendations for the special instruction, behavioral/attention plans, and counseling support that the student needs to strengthen his or her weaker areas. The intervention plan specifies who is responsible for the case management and ensures that all staff and parents are functioning as a team to successfully implement the intervention plan. Finally, the intervention plan specifies how things will be implemented and who is responsible.

Many accommodations allow students with learning challenges to demonstrate their knowledge without being handicapped by the effects of their difficulties. In planning, it is crucial that the teacher consider instructional methods and strategies that either circumvent the student's difficulties or build in the necessary scaffolding to empower the student to be successful with the demands of the assignment.

When advocating for adaptations and accommodations, it is essential for educators, parents, and students to first understand the differences between an adaptation and an accommodation. These definitions will help:

> *Accommodation:* Procedure or enhancement that empowers a person with a disability to complete a task that he or she would otherwise be unable to complete because of his or her disability (Maryland State Department of Education, 1999).
>
> *Adaptation:* Modification to the delivery of instruction or materials used rather than modification in content, as that can affect the fulfillment of curriculum goals (Lenz & Schumaker, 1999).

The decisions regarding adaptations must be individualized for each student. The accommodations that are used in assessments must parallel those that are used in instruction and must be based on student strengths. The accommodations and assessments must provide an equal opportunity for students to demonstrate their knowledge. And, lastly, accommodations must be evaluated often and only those that are effective should be continued.

When considering adaptations and accommodations, the overarching principle is to move students, over time, from dependence to independence. With that in mind, an accommodation that is appropriate at a given point in time may be replaced at a later time with another accommodation that helps the student to be more independent.

Although parents and students must have input into the process, the professionals make the final decisions as to what is appropriate. There must be ongoing communication between parents and all staff who are implementing these plans (Weinfeld et al., 2006).

Students who have learning disabilities may qualify for an Individualized Educational Program (IEP) or a 504 Plan. However, students with ADHD may not qualify for either. Nevertheless, teachers and other professionals who recognize attentional issues in their students can effectively use interventions in the classroom to help address the problems that impact student learning (Silverman et al., 2009).

Teach Students Self-Advocacy Skills

Self-advocacy is when students let others know about who they are and what they need. Ms. Smith meets with Sammy to discuss what it means to be a self-advocate. They discuss the following: Who I Am! (Strengths and Needs); What I Need! (Adaptations and Accommodations); Which Tools Work For Me? (Interventions and Strategies); and How to Get What I Need to Succeed! (Weinfeld et al., 2006). When Sammy is able to articulate his own strengths and needs, he will learn to write a self-advocacy letter and will practice his self-advocacy plan verbally. He will be able to communicate this plan to any adult in and out of the school setting in order to receive appropriate support.

Students need to be empowered, not enabled, as they become involved in their learning. Once they are provided with tools, strategies, and skills for learning, students can successfully develop and use their intellect. Students have responsibilities as learners. In order to be successful, they must recognize and accept both their strengths and needs, and gain an understanding of how they learn (metacognition). Once they are aware of their specific issues, students can become active in learning and practicing strategies for thinking, organization, communication, problem solving, and the use of technology. They are expected to complete assignments, become self-directed, and seek help and support as needed. Learning and practicing strategies for developing self-efficacy (the belief in self) and self-advocacy (the ability to tell others what one needs) make it possible for these students to become risk-takers and lifelong learners. Over time, students develop the skills and maturity that allow them to become partners in making decisions regarding their Individualized Education Programs (IEPs; Weinfeld et al., 2006). For students with ADHD, self-control and self-management may be particularly challenging and, for this reason, the emphasis on taking responsibility for their learning, where possible, is doubly effective.

The social-emotional needs of these students are as important as the educational ones. With few exceptions, social-emotional issues contribute to the lack of achievement. It is important to see whether negative behaviors and attitudes are the result of an inadequate program or personal issues. For some students, placement in an appropriate program that attends to their gifts and offers support for their learning needs will result in a positive turnaround in behavior and attitude. The development of skills and competencies in the social-emotional realm contribute to and complement the other best practices that promote success. Social-emotional health matters inside the classroom and beyond. Students need tools and practice to develop self-efficacy, or the ability to know and to believe in one's self. They need to learn how to say, "I can do this." They need tools and practice for becoming self-advocates, or the ability to know one's self and represent one's self with others. For example, they have to learn to tell an instructor about their needs (e.g., "I am really listening, but I have trouble sitting still. May I get up and quietly walk to the back of the room and then return to my seat?").

The goal is that students see themselves as successful learners by knowing who they are, what they need, which tools work for them, and how to get what they need to succeed. Self-confidence is a critical asset in school success for students with ADHD (Silverman et al., 2009).

Tool 32:
Effective Instruction Checklist

This checklist is a powerful self-evaluation tool for educators.

Tips

Teachers: This checklist represents a summary of best practices in the classroom. It encompasses successful strategies for all students including those with ADHD.

Effective Instruction Checklist

Best Practices

Promote On-Task Performance
- ❏ Teach students the importance of time on task and teach support strategies.
- ❏ Teach students procedural steps to complete the task.
- ❏ Teach students expectations for behavior and classroom standards.
- ❏ Provide students with designated areas in the classroom for supplies, completed assignments, activities, and projects.
- ❏ Provide students with options and alternative activities to work on once they have completed an assigned task.
- ❏ Have students work on activities that are appropriate and have purpose.
- ❏ Introduce tasks in a clear, concise, and interesting way.
- ❏ Observe when students are off task.
- ❏ Use signals and cues to keep students on task.
- ❏ Provide effective and efficient transitions between tasks.
- ❏ Provide a variety of technological tools.

Provide for Student Choice
- ❏ Provide students with opportunities to create and present original ideas and work.
- ❏ Offer students choices in content, process, and product to demonstrate understanding of concepts and content.
- ❏ Provide opportunities for students to initiate discussions and raise questions.
- ❏ Offer an array of technology.

❏ Provide opportunities for students to examine social issues (e.g., bullying, relationships, etc.), develop alternatives, make appropriate choices, and explore effective problem-solving solutions.

Provide a Variety of Resources, Materials, and Tasks Appropriate to the Learning Needs of Individual Students

❏ Offer students a variety of materials to learn and practice concepts.
❏ Vary strategies and activities to convey information.
❏ Provide students with guided practice.
❏ Provide students with independent practice.
❏ Recognize that learning activities vary for individual students.
❏ Make technology available at all times to students.
❏ Use culturally responsive instruction; value differing experiences and cultural perspectives.

Create Cooperative and Flexible Grouping

❏ Plan and implement cooperative learning strategies.
❏ Use peer tutoring and coaching.
❏ Use flexible and heterogeneous grouping.
❏ Utilize technology for student pairs and teams.
❏ Develop an understanding of how student effort, behavior, attitude, and learning style influence group experiences.

Emphasize Process or Strategy-Based Instruction

❏ Teach students how to visualize, verify, predict, and use metacognitive techniques including think aloud.
❏ Emphasize the relationships between and among concepts.
❏ Help students understand and develop relationships between prior knowledge to new information.
❏ Teach students to use graphic organizers and models.
❏ Teach students to use research processes.
❏ Allow think time.
❏ Emphasize higher level questions and thinking.
❏ Teach students to think critically and creatively.
❏ Utilize technology.

Reinforce Student Self-Management and Self-Control

❏ Students plan their own work and select effective and efficient strategies for task completion.
❏ Students monitor their understanding of material by using a variety of strategies including think/pair/share, learning journals, questioning, etc.

Tool 32: Effective Instruction Checklist

❏ Students evaluate their own work using rubrics, checklists, etc.

❏ Students record their assignments and academic progress.

❏ Students monitor their own behavior.

❏ Students use technology.

Maintain Positive Classroom Management

❏ Teacher has consistent expectations for student behavior with appropriate consequences.

❏ Teacher moves around the classroom.

❏ Teacher monitors individual and group behavior.

❏ Teacher maintains high expectations for students and respect for individual differences.

❏ Teacher respects and accepts feelings of students.

❏ Teacher uses positive reinforcement.

❏ Teacher displays a sense of humor.

❏ Teacher provides feedback to students that is timely, specific, and shows appreciation for effective work and support for needed improvement.

❏ Teacher uses technology to record student data.

Provide Instructional Relevance of Evaluation Procedures

❏ Share with students the criteria and rubrics used to grade assignments before starting.

❏ Have students use rubrics to evaluate their own work.

❏ Focus instruction and assessment on concepts and process.

❏ Provide assessments that are meaningful, authentic, performance-based, motivating, and correlate to instructional activities.

❏ Allow students to use alternative products, and demonstrate learning of concepts and content in a variety of ways.

❏ Give students opportunities to self-evaluate.

❏ Give students opportunities to use multimedia technology in performance and assessment.

Use Collaborative Teaching

❏ Teacher also functions as a facilitator in the classroom.

❏ Teach with other teachers in the classroom.

❏ Teacher uses an interdisciplinary approach.

❏ Teacher uses technology with colleagues and experts in and out of the school.

❏ Teacher works in study groups and conducts action research.

❏   Teacher plans collaboratively with special and resource personnel including counselor, speech/language pathologist, gifted and talented teacher,
ESOL teacher, media specialist, technology technician, and more.

Note. Adapted from Montgomery County Public Schools (1998).

Tool 32: Effective Instruction Checklist

Tool 33:
Adaptations and
Accommodations

For students who are gifted and have learning disabilities or ADHD to participate and succeed in enriched and accelerated instruction (gifted, honors, Advanced Placement), they often need to have appropriate adaptations and accommodations (Barton & Starnes, 1989; Baum, 1990; Cline & Schwartz, 1999; National Association for Gifted Children [NAGC], 1998). Many accommodations allow bright students with learning challenges to demonstrate their knowledge without being handicapped by the effects of their difficulties. In planning, it is crucial that the teacher consider instructional methods and strategies that either circumvent the student's difficulties or that build the necessary scaffolding to empower students to be successful with the demands of the assignment.

Tips

Teachers: Use as a self-evaluation and program checklist and when planning for instruction. Use this tool as a communication tool with parents, other staff members, and students.

Adaptations and Accommodations Checklist

Research has revealed that the principles put forth here are the best practices for providing appropriate adaptations and accommodations for kids with learning difficulties or ADHD in order to ensure access to a free and appropriate public education.

❏ Accommodations used in assessments should parallel accommodations that are integrated into classroom instruction (Council for Exceptional Children [CEC], 2000; Maryland State Department of Education [MSDE], 2000).

❏ The adaptations/accommodations are aligned with the educational impact of the individual student's disability and the adaptations/accommodations are aligned with the needs described in the student's IEP or 504 plan (CEC, 2000; MSDE, 2000).

❏ The adaptations/accommodations are based upon the strengths of the student (Baum, 1990; Gardner, 1983; NAGC, 1998).

❑ Accommodations are based on what students need in order to be provided with an equal opportunity to show what they know without impediment of their disability (Thurlow, House, Scott, & Ysseldyke, 2001).

❑ Assessments allow students, while using appropriate accommodations, to demonstrate their skills without interference from their disabilities (CEC, 2000).

❑ After selecting and providing appropriate adaptations/accommodations, their impact on the performance of the individual student is evaluated and only those that are effective are continued (Fuchs, Fuchs, Eaton, Hamlett, & Karns, 2000).

❑ The adaptations/accommodations are reviewed, revised, and when appropriate, faded over time, allowing the student to move from dependence to independence (MSDE, 2000).

❑ A multidisciplinary team, which considers the input of the parent and student, decides upon the adaptations/accommodations (IDEA, 1997; Section 504, 1973).

❑ The appropriate adaptations/accommodations and the rationale for each of them are shared with all staff members who work with the student (IDEA, 1997).

Note. Adapted from Weinfeld et al. (2006).

Tool 33: Adaptations and Accommodations

Tool 34: Adaptations/Accommodations for Overcoming Obstacles Checklist

The following are suggestions for appropriate adaptations and accommodations that circumvent student weaknesses related to the obstacles of writing, organization, reading and memory. They are listed in the following subcategories: Assistive Technology, Instructional Materials, Teaching/Assessment Methods, and Instruct Students in.

Tips

Teachers: Use the checklist when planning and implementing strategies for overcoming obstacles.

Adaptations/Accommodations for Overcoming Obstacles Checklist

Adaptations and Accommodations—Writing

Assistive Technology
- ❏ voice recognition software
- ❏ writing organizational software
- ❏ electronic spellers and dictionaries
- ❏ computer with spelling and grammar checker
- ❏ portable keyboards
- ❏ word prediction software
- ❏ programs that read writing aloud, providing for audio spell checker, proofreading, word prediction, and homophone distinction
- ❏ tape recorder for transcription after student dictation

Instructional Materials
- ❏ step-by-step written directions
- ❏ a proofreading checklist
- ❏ graphic organizers
- ❏ scoring rubric, models, and anchor papers for students to evaluate work
- ❏ guides such as story starters, webs, and outlines

❏ dictionaries, word banks, and thesauri
❏ personal dictionaries of misused and misspelled words
❏ highlighters to indicate errors and corrections
❏ copy of teacher's notes or of another student's notes (NCR paper)
❏ pencil grips and mechanical pencils
❏ paper with raised lines
❏ slant boards

Teaching/Assessment Methods

❏ focus on content rather than mechanics
❏ focus on quality rather than quantity
❏ prepare storyboards, guided imagery, dramatization, or projects before the writing process
❏ set important purposes for writing, such as writing for publication
❏ allow students to write in areas of interest or expertise
❏ allow students to show understanding through alternative products
❏ reduce or alter written requirements
❏ break down assignments into smaller, manageable parts
❏ allow additional time
❏ proofread for one type of error at a time
❏ permit work with partners or small groups during revising, editing, and proofreading
❏ permit students to use words or phrases instead of complete sentences
❏ allow students to make artistic (visual, spatial, and performing) products
❏ allow students to make scientific and technological products
❏ provide dictated response
❏ students review and summarize important information and directions
❏ invite student questions regarding directions and assignments
❏ provide a portfolio assessment of products and performances
❏ allow alternative spelling
❏ provide students with a list of needed materials and their locations

Instruct Students in

❏ the writing process
❏ prewriting strategies, including brainstorming, making a web, and drawing about the topic
❏ rewriting questions into answer form
❏ writing for a variety of purposes
❏ combining words into meaningful sentences
❏ formulating topic sentences
❏ organizing sentences and incorporating adequate details and support statements into paragraphs

Tool 34: Adaptations/Accommodations for Overcoming Obstacles

❑ language conventions (e.g., grammar, punctuation, spelling, usage)
❑ history/structure of language
❑ keyboarding skills

Adaptations and Accommodations—Organization

Assistive Technology
❑ electronic organizers
❑ software organization programs
❑ audiotaping assignments
❑ e-mailing assignments from school to student's home account

Instructional Materials
❑ visual models, storyboards, Venn diagrams, matrices, and flow charts
❑ study guides that help locate information and answers
❑ highlighters, index tabs, and colored stickers
❑ assignment books and calendars for recording assignments
❑ outlines, webs, diagrams, and other graphic organizers

Teaching/Assessment Methods
❑ use short, simple directions
❑ provide advanced organizers regarding what students will know by the end of the lesson
❑ post class and homework assignments in the same area each day and assure that students record them and/or have a printed copy
❑ verbally review class and homework assignments
❑ list and verbally review step-by-step directions for assignments
❑ work with students to establish specific due dates for short-term assignments and time frames for long-term assignments
❑ break up tasks into workable and obtainable steps
❑ encourage study buddies
❑ give examples and specific steps to accomplish tasks
❑ provide checkpoints for long-term assignments and monitor progress frequently
❑ allow students to review and summarize important information and directions
❑ invite student questions regarding directions and assignments
❑ provide students with a list of needed materials and their locations
❑ periodically check notebooks and lockers
❑ provide a homework hotline or structured homework assistance
❑ post a daily routine and explain any changes in that routine
❑ provide an uncluttered work area

- ❏ label and store materials in designated locations
- ❏ provide a specific location for students to place completed work
- ❏ provide samples of finished products

Instruct Students in
- ❏ how to prioritize tasks
- ❏ how to ask questions regarding unclear directions and assignments
- ❏ metacognition
- ❏ how to break long-term assignments into manageable components
- ❏ note taking
- ❏ a routine to follow to prepare for each class
- ❏ a system for organizing notebooks and lockers
- ❏ how to use software organization programs
- ❏ how to use assignment books, calendars, electronic organizers, visual models, and graphic organizers
- ❏ how to access homework help

Adaptations and Accommodations—Reading

Assistive Technology
- ❏ CD-ROMs with audio component
- ❏ electronic spellers that speak words aloud
- ❏ books on tape and digital books
- ❏ computer programs that allow words to be read aloud
- ❏ text-to-speech software

Instructional Materials
- ❏ interviews, speakers, and demonstrations
- ❏ multimedia presentations
- ❏ tape-recorded directions or tests
- ❏ text study guides and graphic organizers to help locate information
- ❏ access to challenging reading programs, like Junior Great Books
- ❏ high-interest, appropriate-level reading material and multilevel texts about the same topic
- ❏ above-grade-level high-interest reading material
- ❏ rich literature experiences
- ❏ expository reading experiences
- ❏ visuals (outlines, graphic organizers, charts, photographs, diagrams, and maps) to help students understand written information
- ❏ word banks

Tool 34: Adaptations/Accommodations for Overcoming Obstacles

Teaching/Assessment Methods

❏ develop interest and curiosity by activating prior knowledge

❏ use a multiple intelligence approach

❏ begin with an experience or project

❏ teach through the arts (drama, visual arts, poetry)

❏ utilize simulations and moral dilemmas

❏ encourage reading related to students' areas of interest

❏ set purposes for reading and state what students should know after reading the text

❏ ask lower level comprehension questions in order to build up to higher level questions

❏ cue students to important words and concepts verbally and through highlighting

❏ teach vocabulary in context

❏ give students the opportunity to read silently before reading aloud

❏ allow students to choose whether or not to read aloud

❏ pair students who have strong decoding skills with weak decoders

❏ allow students to do difficult tasks in small groups

❏ read directions or tests aloud

❏ allow additional time for reading

❏ teach students to outline, underline, or highlight important points

❏ encourage students to take notes while reading

❏ offer support and clarification for imbedded directions in text

Instruct Students in

❏ phonological awareness and phonics

❏ a multisensory reading approach

❏ a rule-based approach to reading

❏ sight vocabulary

❏ prefixes and suffixes

❏ how to use a textbook (i.e., understanding the index, table of contents, glossary, charts, tables, captions, and bold text)

❏ outlining and note taking

Adaptations and Accommodations—Memory

Assistive Technology

❏ software programs as an alternative way of presenting information

❏ tape-recorded directions or information

❏ software programs to organize key points

Instructional Materials

❑ multiple modalities when presenting directions, explanations, and instructional content
❑ those that address multiple learning styles
❑ utilize materials that are meaningful to students
❑ copies of the information that highlight key facts

Teaching/Assessment Methods

❑ have students repeat the directions or information back to teacher
❑ have students repeat information to selves
❑ have students recall important details at the end of a lesson
❑ have students sequence activities after a lesson or event
❑ have students teach information to other students
❑ have students deliver the schedule of events to other students
❑ deliver directions, explanations, and instructional content in a clear manner and at an appropriate pace
❑ provide students with a written list of materials and directions
❑ give auditory and visual cues to help students recall information
❑ provide students with environmental cues and prompts such as posted rules and steps for performing tasks
❑ have students use resources in the environment to recall information (e.g., notes, textbooks, pictures, etc.)
❑ relate information presented to students' previous experiences
❑ have students outline, highlight, underline, or summarize information that should be remembered
❑ repeat information by using different experiences and modalities
❑ provide students with information from a variety of sources
❑ use visual imagery
❑ tell students what to listen for when receiving information

Instruct Students in

❑ transforming information from one modality to another (e.g., from verbal to a diagram or from visual to verbal)
❑ questioning any directions, explanations, and instructions they do not understand
❑ delivering increasingly long verbal messages
❑ how to organize information into smaller units
❑ using sources in the environment to recall information (e.g., notes, pictures)
❑ how to practice memory skills by engaging in activities that are purposeful, such as delivering messages or being in charge of a task
❑ how to highlight and summarize information

- ❑ practicing repetition of information
- ❑ engaging in memory games and activities
- ❑ listening skills
- ❑ visual imagery
- ❑ systematic ways to store and retrieve information
- ❑ how to use advanced organizers, such as lists, tables, and graphics
- ❑ study and test-taking skills
- ❑ routines for beginning a task
- ❑ how to recognize key words

Tools 35–47: What Works/What Doesn't Charts

The following are charts of what works and what doesn't work for kids with learning difficulties.

Tips

Teachers: Use any or all of the following 13 charts as tools when planning for instruction. Use as a communication tool with parents, other staff members, and students (Weinfeld et al., 2006).

Tool 35: What Works/What Doesn't Work: Climate

What Works	What Doesn't Work
✓ Understanding of students' unique strengths and needs ✓ Promoting self-advocacy skills ✓ Comfortable, yet challenging classroom with a stimulating environment—posters, collections, and products displayed ✓ Highly visible class standards and expectations ✓ Student freedom of movement within classroom ✓ Interactive participation ✓ Flexibility ✓ High classroom standards ✓ Cooperative groups ✓ Individualized programming ✓ Conflict resolution instruction ✓ Multimedia resources available ✓ Technological tools available— word processors, calculators, spell checkers	✗ Routine and remedial drill and practice with focus on students' disabilities ✗ Lowering standards ✗ Confrontational communication ✗ Inflexible expectations that diminish student individuality

Tool 36: What Works/What Doesn't Work: Social/Emotional

What Works	What Doesn't Work
✓ Respecting students	✗ Disrespect
✓ Encouragement	✗ Sarcasm
✓ Connecting to students through their strengths and interests	✗ Limiting options and choices
✓ Focusing on strengths, analyzing successes, and applying strengths to weaknesses	✗ Stressing the importance of the weaknesses
✓ Teaching conflict resolution skills	✗ Using negative consequences only
✓ Teaching self-advocacy and self-efficacy	✗ Using one instructional method
✓ Offering choices	✗ Denying access to positive learning experiences
✓ Offering alternative ideas and options	✗ Discipline as punishment only
✓ Extracurricular enrichment activities	✗ Lack of communication
✓ Teaching students to channel frustrations	✗ Fear of being wrong or making mistakes
✓ Easing and removing barriers and planning for the future	
✓ Using nonverbal strategies to support students	
✓ Discipline as a teachable moment	
✓ Encouraging risk taking	
✓ Opportunities to practice skills to build confidence	

Tool 37: What Works/What Doesn't Work: Gifted Instruction

What Works	What Doesn't Work
✓ Studying, knowing, and practicing models for gifted education ✓ Activities that focus on students' gifts and interests ✓ Open-ended outlets for the demonstration of knowledge ✓ Differentiated instruction ✓ Tasks that fit students' learning styles ✓ Multisensory instruction ✓ Support and clarification for directions ✓ Offering students choices ✓ Alternative product options ✓ Collaboratively designed rubrics ✓ Hands-on experiences ✓ Real-life tasks ✓ Integration of visual and performing arts	✗ Remedial instruction ✗ Rigid task guidelines ✗ Belief that GT/LD students can organize their thinking without accommodations or instruction ✗ Perceiving lack of production as a sign of motivational weakness or lower intelligence ✗ Rote memorization ✗ Forced oral reading ✗ Text-based instruction ✗ Only teacher-directed activities (lecture only; activities that do not encourage student decision making or participation)

Tool 38: What Works/What Doesn't Work: Thinking

What Works	What Doesn't Work
✓ Teachers learning thinking strategies ✓ Teaching and modeling thinking strategies ✓ Practicing thinking strategies in the classroom ✓ Applying thinking strategies ✓ Working with GT/LD students to formulate questions, think through problems, use the Socratic method, actively participate in the learning process, apply abstract concepts to everyday occurrences, develop a thinking process, develop a thinking language, or search for their own solutions ✓ Utilizing metacognitive skills ✓ Transferring/applying thinking strategies that work in areas of strengths to areas of need	✗ Assuming students know thinking strategies ✗ Assuming students can apply thinking strategies without ongoing practice

Tool 39: What Works/What Doesn't Work: Reading

What Works	What Doesn't Work
✓ Emphasis on comprehension, and gaining information	✗ Focusing on errors that do not affect comprehension
✓ Using literature for stimulating reading interests	✗ Reading worksheets
✓ High-interest personal reading material	✗ Round-robin reading
✓ Programs like the William and Mary Reading Program that build abstract reasoning and comprehension skills	✗ Categorizing below-grade-level basal readers
✓ Development of expository reading	
✓ Oral discussion using supporting text	
✓ Explicit instruction in phonological awareness, phonics, and decoding (such as that used in Wilson Reading Program)	
✓ Using books on tape and speech-to-text software	

Tool 40: What Works/What Doesn't Work: Writing

What Works	What Doesn't Work
✓ Establishing writing process through ongoing discussion and practice ✓ Assistive technology—portable word processors, computers, electronic spellers, word-predictive software ✓ Graphic organizers ✓ Mind mapping strategies ✓ Extended time for completion of work ✓ Clearly written expectations for writing tasks ✓ Writing prompts ✓ Proofreading for one type of error at a time ✓ Highlighters to indicate corrections ✓ Publication of writing for an audience	✗ Focusing on handwriting instead of content ✗ Quantity versus quality ✗ Using red pens to denote errors

Tool 41: What Works/What Doesn't Work: Organization

What Works	What Doesn't Work
✓ Electronic organizers ✓ Software organization programs ✓ Study guides that help locate information and answers ✓ Assignment books and calendars for recording assignments ✓ Graphic organizers—outlines, webs, diagrams, storyboards ✓ Establishing specific due dates for short-term assignments and time frames for long-term assignments ✓ Breaking down tasks into workable and obtainable steps ✓ Providing checkpoints for long-term assignments and monitoring progress frequently ✓ Providing time to organize materials and assignments ✓ Providing a homework hotline or web page ✓ A specific location for students to place completed work ✓ Monitoring students' accuracy in recording assignments and/or providing printed copy. ✓ Multiple modalities when presenting directions, explanations, and instructional content ✓ Having students sequence activities after a lesson or event	✗ Assuming students have the needed organizational skills ✗ Attributing poor organizational skills to lack of motivation, bad attitude, or laziness ✗ Assigning long-term or complicated assignments without supports for organization ✗ Expecting students to utilize organizational supports without providing instruction in the use of those supports

Tools 35–47: What Works/What Doesn't Charts

Tool 42: What Works/What Doesn't Work: Memory

What Works	What Doesn't Work
✓ Providing students with a copy of the information that highlights key facts ✓ Having students tape record directions or information ✓ Providing students with environmental cues and prompts—posted rules, steps for performing tasks, etc. ✓ Allowing students to use resources in the environment to recall information—notes, textbooks, pictures, etc. ✓ Relating information to students' previous experiences ✓ Having students outline, highlight, underline, or summarize information that should be remembered ✓ Telling students what to listen for when being given directions or receiving information ✓ Associative cues or mnemonic devices ✓ Teaching visual imagery	✗ Using only one modality, such as a lecture, to teach a lesson ✗ Expecting students to recall facts without support ✗ Expecting students to utilize mnemonics, visual imagery, technology, or other supports without teaching them how to use these tools

Tool 43: What Works/What Doesn't Work: Handwriting

What Works	What Doesn't Work
✓ Focusing on form ✓ Mechanical pencils or grips ✓ Appropriate handwriting program ✓ Assistive technology	✗ Lengthy handwriting tasks that result in fatigue ✗ Expectations that disregard students' physical weaknesses or limitations

Tool 44: What Works/What Doesn't Work: Math

What Works	What Doesn't Work
✓ Preassessment of students' mastery of mathematical categories (e.g., decimals, fractions, whole numbers, statistics and probability, etc.) ✓ Preassessment of students' mastery of mathematical objectives ✓ Focusing on developing conceptual skills and problem-solving strategies ✓ A multidisciplinary approach ✓ Interactive approach ✓ Hands-on programs ✓ Manipulatives ✓ Untimed tests if indicated ✓ Reduction in number of problems ✓ Direct instruction for the use of calculators	✗ Lengthy assignments ✗ Repetitive assignments ✗ Copying from the textbook, overheads, or blackboard ✗ Focusing on computation alone

Tool 45: What Works/What Doesn't Work: Science

What Works	What Doesn't Work
✓ Hands-on, interactive experiences ✓ Activities that incorporate problem solving and real-life investigations with a purpose and an end product ✓ Thematic approach that allows for students to direct their search for knowledge and answers ✓ Simulations ✓ Integration of visual and performing arts ✓ Focus on science process objectives ✓ Graphic organizers to support note taking	✗ Instruction led by textbook reading ✗ Focusing on facts rather than understanding concepts

Tool 46: What Works/What Doesn't Work: Social Studies

What Works	What Doesn't Work
✓ Holding students accountable for learning the historical, economic, political, geographic, and cultural content standards ✓ Constructing understandings through systems of processing information, critical thinking, and problem solving ✓ Thematic units ✓ Simulations ✓ Hands-on activities and projects ✓ Using various forms of media ✓ Integration of visual and performing arts ✓ Extension/enrichment activities	✗ Instruction led by textbook reading ✗ Focusing on facts rather than understanding concepts

Tool 47: What Works/What Doesn't Work: Evaluations and Assessments

What Works	What Doesn't Work
✓ Student/teacher collaboration on the evaluation and assessment methods and tools ✓ Evaluations based on instruction reflecting the key concepts and basic understandings of the curriculum ✓ Providing objectives, study guides, vocabulary, acceptable responses, support, and clarification for questions ✓ Differentiation ✓ Audiotape responses ✓ Graphic organizers in lieu of paragraph responses ✓ Creating a model ✓ Giving a speech	✗ Lengthy essays ✗ Penalties for spelling in content areas ✗ Time limits ✗ Matching tasks

Tools 48–53:
Bordering on Excellence Tools

The Bordering on Excellence tools drive theory to practice by helping teachers tailor instruction for each student.

They interface with any instructional material and will allow educators to consider the multiple issues that they need to effectively and efficiently address when differentiating content, process, and product.

The components are:

✓ **Frame of Reference:** This is a desk and/or notebook reference companion designed to address the differentiated needs and expertise of staff. It is useful for training and teacher/parent conferences. It includes two sections: Big Picture and Possible Stumbling Blocks. (Refer to Adaptations and Accommodations for Overcoming Obstacles Checklist on pp. 72–78 for more information). Simply reproduce or copy the pages that follow into a format that suits you best, whether it is several two-sided cards or a packet of information.

✓ **Bordering on Excellence Frame:** A blank frame that provides an alternative format for analyzing either the needs of specific students or evaluating the obstacles inherent in a lesson. It is useful for training and teacher/parent conferences. We have provided examples for you to follow, along with blank frames for each of the four trouble areas faced by smart kids with learning difficulties or ADHD. These frames can also be used to evaluate instructional materials, including curricular guides, books, teacher-made study guides, and workbooks (Weinfeld et al., 2006).

✓ **Sample Completed Frames**: These frames show two examples of how the Bordering on Excellence tools may be used.

Tips

Teachers: Use the collection of tools as references, for planning purposes, as a student record form, with instructional materials to obviate student weaknesses and tap strengths, and as a communication tool with parents, other staff members, and students.

Tool 48: Bordering on Excellence Frame of Reference

The Big Picture

Ensure
- ✓ Focus on strengths and interests
- ✓ Instructional adaptations and accommodations
- ✓ Comprehensive case management

Teach
- ✓ Decoding skills
- ✓ Writing process
- ✓ Language conventions (e.g., spelling, grammar, punctuation, usage)
- ✓ Note taking
- ✓ Highlighting
- ✓ Outlining
- ✓ Summarizing
- ✓ Prioritizing tasks
- ✓ Organizing materials
- ✓ Keyboarding
- ✓ Word processing

Provide
- ✓ Acceleration and enrichment
- ✓ Open-ended tasks
- ✓ Real-life applications
- ✓ Realistic simulations
- ✓ Emphasis on problem solving, reasoning, and critical thinking
- ✓ Opportunities for student choice
- ✓ Alternative product options
- ✓ Integration of the arts
- ✓ Approach that teaches to various learning styles
- ✓ Opportunities to create authentic products
- ✓ Multisensory approach to learning
- ✓ Flexibility in classroom organization

Possible Stumbling Blocks

Writing
- ✓ the physical act of putting words on paper
- ✓ handwriting

✓ generating topics
✓ combining words into meaningful sentences
✓ organizing sentences and incorporating adequate details and support statements into organized paragraphs
✓ revising and editing
✓ using language mechanics effectively (e.g., grammar, punctuation, spelling)

Organization
✓ following multistep directions
✓ planning the steps needed to complete a task
✓ organizing desk, locker, notebook, and other materials
✓ locating needed materials
✓ breaking long-range assignments into manageable steps
✓ prioritizing

Reading
✓ decoding unfamiliar words
✓ inferring meaning of new words
✓ summarizing
✓ reading fluently and quickly
✓ using textbooks

Memory
✓ concentrating and keeping track of information
✓ quickly recalling details
✓ retrieving details after time has passed

Tool 49: Blank Frame for Writing

Adaptations/Accommodations
Writing

Possible Stumbling Blocks

- ✓ the physical act of putting words on paper
- ✓ handwriting
- ✓ generating topics
- ✓ formulating topic sentences

- ✓ combining words into meaningful sentences
- ✓ using language mechanics effectively (e.g., grammar, punctuation, spelling)

- ✓ organizing sentences and incorporating adequate details and support statements into organized paragraphs
- ✓ revising and editing

Instructional Materials

- ✓ step-by-step written directions
- ✓ a proofreading checklist
- ✓ scoring rubrics, models, and anchor papers for students to evaluate their own work
- ✓ graphic organizers
- ✓ guides such as story starters, webs, story charts, outlines
- ✓ dictionaries, word banks, and thesauri
- ✓ personal dictionaries of misused and misspelled words
- ✓ highlighter to indicate errors/corrections
- ✓ copy of teacher notes or of another student's notes (NCR paper)
- ✓ pencil grips
- ✓ paper with raised lines
- ✓ mechanical pencils
- ✓ slant board

NOTES:

Teaching/Assessment Methods

- ✓ focus on content rather than mechanics
- ✓ focus on quality rather than quantity
- ✓ begin with storyboards, guided imagery, dramatization, or projects before the writing process
- ✓ set important purposes for writing, such as writing for publication, writing to an expert, or writing to a famous person
- ✓ allow students to write in area of interest or expertise
- ✓ allow students to demonstrate understanding through alternative methods/products
- ✓ reduce or alter written requirements
- ✓ break down assignments into smaller, manageable parts
- ✓ additional time
- ✓ work with partners or small groups to confer for revising, editing, and proofreading

Assistive Technology

- ✓ voice recognition software
- ✓ organizational software
- ✓ electronic spellers and dictionaries
- ✓ tape recorder for student dictation and then transcription

- ✓ computer word processor with spelling and grammar checker or talking word processor
- ✓ portable keyboards
- ✓ word prediction software

- ✓ programs that allow writing to be read aloud
- ✓ programs that provide for audio spell checker, word prediction, and homophone distinction

Tool 50: Blank Frame for Reading

Adaptations/Accommodations
Reading

Possible Stumbling Blocks

- ✓ decoding unfamiliar words
- ✓ inferring meaning of new words
- ✓ summarizing
- ✓ reading fluently and quickly
- ✓ using textbooks

Instructional Materials

- ✓ interviews, guest speakers, and demonstrations
- ✓ multimedia presentations
- ✓ tape-recorded directions or tests
- ✓ text study guides and graphic organizers to help students locate information
- ✓ above-grade-level high-interest reading material
- ✓ high-interest, appropriate-level reading material

NOTES:

Teaching/ Assessment Methods

- ✓ develop interest and curiosity by activating prior knowledge before reading
- ✓ teach through the arts (drama, visual arts, poetry)
- ✓ encourage reading related to students' areas of interest
- ✓ ask lower level comprehension questions in order to build up to higher level questions
- ✓ teach vocabulary in context
- ✓ allow students to choose whether or not to read aloud
- ✓ allow students to do vocabulary webs, literature webs, and other difficult tasks in small groups
- ✓ teach students to outline, underline, or highlight important points in reading

Assistive Technology

- ✓ CD-ROMs with audio component
- ✓ electronic spellers that speak words aloud
- ✓ books on tape and digital books
- ✓ computer programs that allow words to be read aloud
- ✓ text-to-speech software

Tool 51: Blank Frame for Organization

Adaptations/Accommodations
Organization

Possible Stumbling Blocks

- ✓ following multistep directions
- ✓ planning the steps needed to complete a task

- ✓ organizing desk, locker, notebook, and other materials
- ✓ locating needed materials

- ✓ breaking long-range assignments into manageable steps
- ✓ prioritizing

Instructional Materials

- ✓ visual models, storyboards, Venn diagrams, matrices, and flow charts
- ✓ study guides that assist with locating information and answers
- ✓ highlighters, index tabs, and colored stickers
- ✓ assignment books and calendars for recording assignments
- ✓ outlines, webs, diagrams, and other graphic organizers

NOTES:

Teaching/ Assessment Methods

- ✓ use short, simple directions
- ✓ post class and homework assignments in the same area each day and assure that students record them and/or have a printed copy
- ✓ verbally review class and homework assignments
- ✓ work with students to establish specific due dates for short-term assignments and time frames for long-term assignments
- ✓ break down tasks into workable and obtainable steps
- ✓ provide checkpoints for long-term assignments and monitor progress frequently
- ✓ provide homework hotline or structured homework assistance
- ✓ provide a specific location for students to place completed work

Assistive Technology

- ✓ electronic organizers
- ✓ software organization programs

- ✓ audiotaping assignments

- ✓ e-mailing assignments from school to student's home account

Tools 48–53: Bordering on Excellence Tools

Tool 52: Blank Frame for Memory

Adaptations/Accommodations
Memory

Possible Stumbling Blocks

✓ concentrating and keeping track of information

✓ quickly recalling details

✓ retrieving details after time has passed

Instructional Materials	NOTES:	Teaching/ Assessment Methods
✓ use multiple modalities when presenting directions, explanations, and instructional content ✓ provide students with copies of the information that highlight key facts ✓ use materials that are meaningful to students ✓ address multiple learning styles		✓ have students repeat the directions or information back to teacher ✓ have students recall important details at the end of a lesson or period of time ✓ have students teach information to other students ✓ deliver directions, explanations, and instructional content clearly ✓ provide students with environmental cues and prompts such as posted rules and steps for performing tasks ✓ provide students with written list of materials and directions ✓ give auditory and visual cues to help students to recall information ✓ provide adequate opportunities for repetition of information through different experiences and modalities

Assistive Technology

✓ teachers use software programs as an alternative or additional way of presenting information

✓ students tape record directions or information

✓ students use software programs for organization of key points

Tool 53: Sample Completed Frames for Writing and Reading

Adaptations/Accommodations
Writing

Possible Stumbling Blocks

- ✓ the physical act of putting words on paper
- ✓ handwriting
- ✓ generating topics
- ✓ formulating topic sentences
- ✓ combining words into meaningful sentences
- ✓ using language mechanics effectively (e.g., grammar, punctuation, spelling)
- ✓ organizing sentences and incorporating adequate details and support statements into organized paragraphs
- ✓ revising and editing

Instructional Materials

- ✓ step-by-step written directions
- ✓ a proofreading checklist
- ✓ scoring rubrics, models, and anchor papers for students to evaluate their own work
- ✓ graphic organizers
- ✓ guides such as story starters, webs, story charts, outlines
- ✓ dictionaries, word banks, and thesauri
- ✓ personal dictionaries of misused and misspelled words
- ✓ highlighter to indicate errors/corrections
- ✓ copy of teacher notes or of another student's notes (NCR paper)
- ✓ pencil grips
- ✓ paper with raised lines
- ✓ mechanical pencils
- ✓ slant board

NOTES:

–5 students with difficulties in writing

–written production required
- literature webs (2 chapters)
- vocabulary webs (2 words)
- change matrix with specific evidence
- written reflections

–I will need to address the following:
- stumbling blocks (circled)
- interventions (circled)
- technology (circled)

–make sure students have access to computers/software

–concerned with Johnny
- great ideas, but poor production
- doesn't have good computer skills
- needs to be able to dictate ideas on tape or to an adult for transcription
- needs to be able to use computer with word-predictive software

Teaching/Assessment Methods

- ✓ focus on content rather than mechanics
- ✓ focus on quality rather than quantity
- ✓ begin with storyboards, guided imagery, dramatization, or projects before the writing process
- ✓ set important purposes for writing, such as writing for publication, writing to an expert, or writing to a famous person
- ✓ allow students to write in area of interest or expertise
- ✓ allow students to demonstrate understanding through alternative methods/products
- ✓ reduce or alter written requirements
- ✓ break down assignments into smaller, manageable parts
- ✓ additional time
- ✓ work with partners or small groups to confer for revising, editing, and proofreading

Assistive Technology

- ✓ voice recognition software
- ✓ organizational software
- ✓ electronic spellers and dictionaries
- ✓ tape recorder for student dictation and then transcription
- ✓ computer word processor with spelling and grammar checker or talking word processor
- ✓ portable keyboards
- ✓ word prediction software
- ✓ programs that allow writing to be read aloud
- ✓ programs that provide for audio spell checker, word prediction, and homophone distinction

Adaptations/Accommodations
Reading

Possible Stumbling Blocks

✓ decoding unfamiliar words
✓ inferring meaning of new words
✓ summarizing
✓ reading fluently and quickly
✓ using textbooks

Instructional Materials

✓ interviews, guest speakers, and demonstrations
✓ multimedia presentations
✓ tape-recorded directions or tests
✓ text study guides and graphic organizers to help students locate information
✓ above-grade-level high-interest reading material
✓ high-interest, appropriate-level reading material

NOVEL ASSIGNMENT:

– All students read

_____ by
_____.

– Students choose one other novel:
• _____
• _____
• _____
• _____
• _____

– Activities:
• Create a literature web for two chapters from each of the novels. Include the following: structure, feelings, ideas, other (choose two additional terms to explore on your web).
• Make a list of vocabulary words that reflect main character traits from each novel.
• Create a Venn diagram that reflects the similarities and differences between the two novels.

Teaching/ Assessment Methods

✓ develop interest and curiosity by activating prior knowledge before reading
✓ teach through the arts (drama, visual arts, poetry)
✓ encourage reading related to students' areas of interest
✓ ask lower level comprehension questions in order to build up to higher level questions
✓ teach vocabulary in context
✓ allow students to choose whether or not to read aloud
✓ allow students to do vocabulary webs, literature webs, and other difficult tasks in small groups
✓ teach students to outline, underline, or highlight important points in reading

Assistive Technology

✓ CD-ROMs with audio component
✓ electronic spellers that speak words aloud
✓ books on tape and digital books
✓ computer programs that allow words to be read aloud
✓ text-to-speech software

Tool 54:
Memory Strategies

Students with ADHD may have difficulty concentrating, keeping track of information, recalling details quickly, sequencing details, and retrieving details over time. Teaching specific strategies to students may be extremely helpful for enhancing memory. The more strategies they can learn and practice, the better able they are to find those that are best suited to their needs.

Tips

Teachers and Parents: Offer these strategies to students who have difficulty remembering information. By practicing each strategy, students will find those that best suit their learning style. These strategies become part of a "bag of tricks" to choose from to better ensure school success.

Memory Strategies

A mnemonic device aids memory by creating a connection between something that is easy to remember and something that is hard to remember. There are many suggested mnemonic devices. Some examples are:

1. Create a word you know from the first letters of a list of words or ideas you must remember.

   Example: You must remember the Great Lakes: Heron, Superior, Ontario, Michigan, Erie.
   Mnemonic device: HOMES = Heron, Ontario, Michigan Erie, Superior

2. Create a song to make a connection to the information you need to remember.

   Example: You must remember a phone number.
   Mnemonic device: Create a song you can sing that is made from the phone number. Sing it over and over to help you remember the number.

3. Visualize a picture that connects the information you must remember to what you see in your mind.

    Example: You must remember to take your backpack to school each day.

    Mnemonic device: Close your eyes and visualize your backpack at the front door of your home before you leave each morning.

4. Choose any object and connect it to what you must remember.

    Example: You must remember Abraham Lincoln and Jefferson Davis and the Civil War.

    Mnemonic device: Take each idea and connect it to your object. The stranger the object, the easier it may be to remember. Picture a horse skateboarding between Abraham Lincoln in the North to Jefferson Davis in the South during the Civil War.

5. Put the information you need to remember into categories.

    Example: You must remember ingredients for a recipe to buy at the store.

    Mnemonic device: Put eggs, flour, milk, chocolate chips, and sugar into categories. Wet: eggs, milk and Dry: flour, chocolate chips, sugar

6. Create a statement related to a symbol.

    Example: You must remember the difference between the "less than" and "greater than" mathematical symbols: < and >

    Mnemonic device: The open area "eats" the larger number. $3 < 6$; $12 > 2$

Tool 55:
Self-Advocacy

Self-advocacy is when students let others know about who they are and what they need. Learning and practicing strategies for developing self-advocacy make it possible for these students to become risk-takers and lifelong learners. Over time, students develop the skills and maturity that allow them to become partners in decision making regarding their Individualized Education Programs.

Tips

Teachers: Use this tool with students to help them identify their strengths and needs. Collaborate with students so you both gain an understanding of strengths and needs. Provide an opportunity for students to practice their self-advocacy skills (e.g., role-playing, simulations).

Self-Advocacy
What Defines Me as a Successful Learner?

Who I am (strengths and needs):

_____

_____

_____

_____

_____

What I need (adaptations and accommodations):

_____

_____

_____

_____

_____

Which tools work for me (interventions and strategies)?

_____

_____

_____

_____

_____

How to get what I need to succeed:

_____

_____

_____

_____

_____

Tool 55: Self-Advocacy

Tool 56:
Parent and Student Interview

When the focus of learning is on students' strengths and interests, rather than areas of weakness, then self-confidence and self-esteem are increased and students are more likely to be successful. Interviews are one way to obtain information on student strengths and interests.

Tips

Teachers: Use the Parent Interview questions to gain information about the student. Use the Student Interview questions to help you identify your student's strengths and interests. When planning instruction for the student, work through these strengths whenever possible. The questions also are helpful when trying to match your student with a mentor.

Parent and Student Interview

Parent Interview

1. What does your child choose to do in his or her free time?

2. What are your child's interests in school?

3. What are your child's interests outside of school?

4. What are your child's hobbies?

5. On what type of school projects is your child most successful?

6. What do you see as your child's strengths, abilities, or expertise?

7. What does your child like to talk about?

8. What does your child read about?

9. How does your child choose to show what he or she knows?

Student Interview

1. What do you choose to do in your free time?

2. What are your interests in school?

3. What are your interests outside of school?

4. What are your hobbies?

5. On what type of school projects are you most successful?

6. What do you see as your strengths, abilities, or areas of expertise?

7. What do you like to talk about?

8. What do you read about?

9. How do you choose to show what you know?

10. If you could study anything that you wanted, what would you choose to study?

11. How did you become interested in this topic?

Tool 56: Parent and Student Interview

12. What have you done on your own (outside of school) in this area?

13. Would you like to work with a mentor (someone who helps you work on projects that interest you)? What is it about working with a mentor that appeals to you?

14. If you could study the topic from Question 10 with a mentor, what types of things are you interested in having a mentor do with you on this topic?

15. How do you like to learn? (For example, do you learn best through books, movies, museums, hands-on experiences, interviewing people, or other methods?)

16. What type of product do you like to develop best? (For example, do you prefer to do an essay, a poster, a movie, a PowerPoint presentation, a model, a speech, or another type of product?)

Tool 57:
How ADHD Feels to Me

We often prescribe interventions to children based on their behaviors but never ask what they experience prior to assessment and treatment. The following tool is designed to get a child's input into his or her own experiences.

Tips

Teachers and Parents: Provide this checklist to the child and add the information to round out the profile.

How ADHD Feels to Me

- ❏ My mind is racing all of the time.
- ❏ I say or do the wrong thing before I think about it.
- ❏ I have to ask my classmates or the teacher what the assignment was because I wasn't paying attention or can't "get it" in class.
- ❏ When I try to copy from the board I make mistakes or forget what I was writing.
- ❏ When I try to write down what the teacher says, I forget much of it.
- ❏ I feel nervous a lot of the time.
- ❏ I feel depressed a lot of the time.
- ❏ I like to count things a lot.
- ❏ I like to be super clean a lot.
- ❏ Everything around me needs to stay in order.
- ❏ I can't help making a mess wherever I go.
- ❏ My room is a total mess.
- ❏ I have all kinds of stuff collecting in my desk.
- ❏ The slightest sound disturbs me when I try to concentrate.
- ❏ I find it really hard to stay on one task for a long time.
- ❏ I need to get up and move when I try to concentrate.
- ❏ I love thrills and taking chances.
- ❏ I prefer to be in motion most of the time.
- ❏ I get bored very easily.
- ❏ I don't have much patience for what people are saying and either don't listen or cut them off when they are talking to me.
- ❏ I need to be busy all the time.
- ❏ My mind is always filled with thoughts even when I'm trying to be calm.

❏ I can't wait to get out of classes or school every day.

❏ I don't have the patience to read long things.

❏ My friends don't have a lot of patience for me because I act immaturely.

❏ I feel pressure when I talk and can't get the words out fast enough.

❏ I get emotionally excited very easily.

❏ I argue a lot.

❏ When I am asked to do something I want to do the opposite or just to refuse to do it.

❏ I play around and act silly most of the time. I am the class clown.

Tool 57: How ADHD Feels to Me

Tool 58:
Action Plan for Educators

The following is an Action Plan designed for educators. There are four pieces: training, collaborative formulation of educational plans, ongoing communication, and evaluation. Each of these components is crucial if effective adaptations and accommodations are to be provided to students with ADHD.

Tips

Teachers: Use the Action Plan to help address your areas of need as a teacher of students with ADHD.

Action Plan for Educators

1. Conduct training for special educators and general educators on:
   a. the definition, identification, and best practices in programming for students with ADHD;
   b. understanding the assessment data that relates to these students;
   c. understanding appropriate resources, materials, strategies, and techniques to be utilized both in instruction and assessments that allow students to demonstrate their skills without the interference of their disabilities;
   d. understanding how to capitalize on students' strengths; and
   e. the need to evaluate and revise adaptations and accommodations.

2. Include general educators as part of the IEP, 504 Plan, or child study team while formulating adaptations and accommodations.
3. Schedule ongoing face-to-face meetings between special educators and general educators to plan for implementation of the student's IEP/504 plan, including needed adaptations and accommodations. Meetings should include a discussion of the reason for each adaptation and accommodation as it relates to the individual student's disability.
4. Build in an evaluation component to look at the efficacy of each adaptation and accommodation with a plan of fading them out over time, allowing students to move from dependence to independence.

Note. Adapted from Weinfeld et al. (2006).

Tool 59:
Action Plan for Parents

The following is an Action Plan designed for teachers to work with parents. There are four pieces: training, collaborative formulation of educational plans, ongoing communication, and evaluation. Each of these components is crucial if effective adaptations and accommodations are to be provided to students with ADHD.

Tips

Teachers: Use the Action Plan with parents.

Action Plan for Parents

1. Conduct training for parents on:
    a. the definition, identification, and best practices in programming for these students;
    b. the possible negative effects of providing excessive or unnecessary accommodations;
    c. the need to select accommodations based on the impact of the individual student's disability;
    d. the need to move students from dependence to independence; and
    e. the need to evaluate and revise adaptations and accommodations.

2. Include parents as part of the IEP, 504 Plan, or child study team, while formulating adaptations and accommodations.
3. Schedule ongoing face-to-face meetings between special educators and parents to monitor implementation of the student's plan, including needed adaptations and accommodations.
4. Build in an evaluation component to look at the efficacy of each adaptation and accommodation with a plan of fading them out over time, allowing students to move from dependence to independence.

Note. Adapted from Weinfeld et al. (2006).

Tool 60:
Action Plan for Students

The following is an Action Plan designed for students. There are four pieces: training, collaborative formulation of educational plans, ongoing communication, and evaluation. Each of these components is crucial if effective adaptations and accommodations are to be provided to students with ADHD.

Tips

Teachers: Use the Action Plan with students.

Action Plan for Students

1. Conduct training for students on:
   a. understanding their own unique strengths and weaknesses;
   b. understanding how specific adaptations/accommodations maximize their strengths, while minimizing their weaknesses;
   c. understanding and implementing advocacy and communication strategies; and
   d. understanding the need to move from dependence to independence.

2. Include students as part of the IEP, 504 Plan, or child study team in the formulation of adaptations and accommodations.
3. Schedule ongoing face-to-face meetings between special educators and students to monitor implementation of the student's plan, including needed adaptations and accommodations.
4. Ensure student participation in a periodic evaluation component to look at the efficacy of each adaptation and accommodation with a plan of fading them out over time, allowing students to move from dependence to independence.

Note. Adapted from Weinfeld et al. (2006).

Tool 61:
Written Work Checklist

Checklists are effective tools to use with students to evaluate written work.

Tips

Teachers: The following checklist may be used as is or adapted to specific assignments.

Written Work Checklist

Content
✓ Does the report contain enough information?   _____
✓ Are the facts accurate?   _____

Construction and Style
✓ Do the title and opening paragraph arouse the
   reader's interest?   _____
✓ Is each paragraph constructed around one idea?   _____
✓ Are your sentences varied to avoid monotony?   _____
✓ Have you capitalized properly?   _____
✓ Have you punctuated properly?   _____

Form
✓ Does your paper have a heading?   _____
✓ Is there a title? Is it capitalized properly?   _____
✓ Are there margins at the left and right?   _____
✓ Is your name on the paper? Are the pages numbered?   _____
✓ Is the first line of each paragraph indented?   _____
✓ Is the penmanship legible? Is the paper neat?   _____
✓ Did you proofread for errors? Are they corrected?   _____

Tool 62:
Writing Skills Rubric

Rubrics are effective tools to use with students to evaluate written work.

Tips

Teachers: The following rubric may be used as is or adapted to specific assignments.

Writing Skills Rubric

1 = Minimum 2 = Satisfactory 3 = Very Good 4 = Outstanding

Ideas and Development   1 2 3 4
- ✓ The written work reflects clear thinking and planning.
- ✓ The written work is an appropriate response to the prompt.

Organization   1 2 3 4
- ✓ The organization is appropriate for the response to the prompt.
- ✓ There is a clear introduction, body, and conclusion.
- ✓ There are transitions between paragraphs.

Voice   1 2 3 4
- ✓ The writer's voice is individual and engaging.
- ✓ The reader senses the person behind the words.
- ✓ The writer's words cause a reaction in the reader.

Word Choice   1 2 3 4
- ✓ The writer's word selection and usage are clear.
- ✓ The writer uses vivid language and active verbs to enhance meaning.

Sentence Fluency   1 2 3 4
- ✓ Sentences vary in both structure and length and include both compound and complex sentences.
- ✓ Dependent clauses help vary the sentence structure.

Conventions

1   2   3   4

✓ Spelling is correct.
✓ Punctuation is correct.
✓ Capitalization is correct.

Total: _____
Grade: _____

Tool 63:
Differentiation

Instruction, when it is differentiated, better matches an individual's abilities, styles, and needs. Differentiation is a way of thinking and planning in order to meet the diverse needs of students based on their characteristics.

Tips

Teachers: This is not a complete list, but rather a starting point. After your research, add whatever you wish that will ensure success for your students.

Differentiation

- ❏ Use a variety of assessments to discover what students know. Use test data, pretests, writing samples, discussion, observation, alternative products, and parent and student input.
- ❏ Provide positive expectations and respect for individual differences.
- ❏ Provide for ongoing communication.
- ❏ Support strength-based instruction in content, process, and product.
- ❏ Provide for acceleration and enrichment.
- ❏ Provide appropriate adaptations and accommodations.
- ❏ Integrate basic skills and higher level questioning and thinking in the curriculum.
- ❏ Provide opportunities for critical and creative thinking.
- ❏ Provide a variety of classroom resources and materials with a variety of levels of difficulty.
- ❏ Provide flexible grouping.
- ❏ Provide for guided and independent work.
- ❏ Offer a variety of activities.
- ❏ Provide for alternative products to allow students to show what they know.
- ❏ Allow for student choice.
- ❏ Allow students to make decisions about creating and presenting original topics.
- ❏ Use a variety of assistive technology.
- ❏ Allow students to manage and develop self-control over their own learning.
- ❏ Help students monitor and evaluate their own work.
- ❏ Use varied, stimulating, and performance-based assessments.

Tool 64:
Collaborative Problem Solving

A collaborative team approach is helpful in developing effective plans and solutions.

Tips

Teachers: Collaborative problem solving should be the style of problem solving in every situation, where professionals and consumers (children and parents) are physically present or in contact through speakerphone or e-mail.

Collaborative Problem Solving

✓ Community agencies, where appropriate, should be involved in meetings.
✓ Students should be involved in the collaborative process, especially at IEP and 504 meetings so that they can take "ownership" of each part of their educational plan.
✓ Each person at a decision table might have her name on a sign in front of her with her function/role.
✓ Although voting on decisions is not necessary, each participant should be polled at the end of a decision to substantiate who is and who is not on board with a solution.
✓ Those who disagree should have an opportunity to express their disagreement and file a grievance appropriately.
✓ Legal differences of opinion should have clear options for mediation or appeal.

Tool 65:
Cueing Checklist

Cueing (i.e., providing a signal, such as a word or action, to prompt on-task behavior) may help students with ADHD compensate for their deficits.

Tips

Teachers: The following checklist offers specific strategies to use during classroom instruction and activities.

Cueing Checklist

- ❏ Use phrases including: "This is important." "Write this information down." "Put this in your notebook." "Record this on your assignment sheet."
- ❏ Privately establish nonintrusive visual cues (e.g., thumb up, touch desk, sticky notes on desk) that will remind the student to stay on task.
- ❏ Use a variety of sound signals (e.g., clap, bell) to indicate transitions or the need to focus attention.
- ❏ Use a tactile approach (e.g., touch shoulder of student).
- ❏ Use a highlighter to cue important information on written material.
- ❏ Use visual supports (e.g., chart, diagram) to reinforce information given verbally.
- ❏ Point to information on the board to reinforce its importance.
- ❏ Change your voice for emphasis (e.g., volume, pitch, pace).
- ❏ Use the student's name first when asking a direct question.
- ❏ Use cue cards to elicit appropriate responses.
- ❏ Ask the student to repeat directions and steps.

Tool 65: Cueing Checklist

Tool 66:
Proximity Checklist

Having a teacher nearby provides a reminder for a student to engage in on-task behavior.

Tips

Teachers: The following checklist offers specific strategies to use during classroom instruction and activities.

Proximity Checklist

❏ Stand close to the student when teaching.
❏ Walk around the room, rather than standing only at the front, in order to keep a student's attention.
❏ Allow the student to sit in front of the class or in a location that offers the least amount of external stimuli.
❏ Designate specific work areas in addition to the student's desk.

Tool 67:
Working With Others Checklist

Students with ADHD often experience rejection and can benefit from interacting with other students in pairs and groups.

Tips

Teachers: The following checklist offers specific strategies to use during classroom instruction and activities.

Working With Others Checklist

❏ Offer collaborative learning opportunities to engage students and increase achievement.

❏ Pair students with ADHD with partners during learning activities.

❏ Use think-pair-share strategies.

❏ Allow students with ADHD opportunities to tutor other students in order to reinforce concepts and content material.

❏ Use cooperative learning strategies in every content area of the curriculum.

❏ Provide reinforcement for on-task behavior during group activities.

❏ Provide social skills instruction to the entire class and provide opportunities for positive social interaction.

❏ Provide conflict resolution instruction to the entire class and provide opportunities for positive responses to conflict.

Tool 68:
Teaching Comprehension

Students with ADHD often need additional assistance with basic comprehension of information.

Tips

Teachers: Use the strategies below to help increase student comprehension of lesson concepts. Direct the student to the significant main ideas to be sought in reading passages or listening by taking notes, using a highlighter. Seat the student close to the source of information. Reduce distractibility around the student.

Teaching Comprehension

- ✓ Practice listening for key facts by asking the student to repeat them.
- ✓ Have students practice inferential thinking through logical sequences.
- ✓ Ask the student what was going on in a TV show or movie.
- ✓ Ask the student to describe pivotal elements in a story by recalling important portions where events changed.
- ✓ Have students practice judging the relevancy of information through embedded distracters.
- ✓ Ask the student to predict what may happen next in a lesson story sequence.
- ✓ Ask the student to recall sequences of detail in a story or visual presentation.
- ✓ Ask the student to identify self-contradictions in a presentation.
- ✓ Help the student to find similarities through classification of items.
- ✓ Practice understanding through practical judgment for decision making in commonplace life experiences necessary for survival such as: "What would you do if?" or "What do we do when?"
- ✓ Ask the student to reconstruct events by rearranging them in sequential order.
- ✓ Help the student differentiate fact from opinion.
- ✓ Ask the student to identify supporting details.
- ✓ Ask the student to arrange events from a story in sequential order.
- ✓ Teach the student to perceive differences between similarly worded statements.

✓ Teach the student to resist the influence of emotion-laden words and arguments.

✓ Motivate the student to develop curiosity and higher interest.

✓ Teach the student to judge relevancy of information.

✓ Teach the student to recognize the topic sentences and to associate each topic sentence with some previous bit of knowledge.

✓ Teach the student to recognize what the speaker wants the listener to do.

✓ Teach the student how words can create a mood.

✓ Teach the student to understand connotative meanings

✓ Teach the student to understand denotative meanings.

✓ Teach the student to identify speaker attitudes.

✓ Teach the student to get meaning from imagery.

✓ Ask the student to check on accuracy of new information.

✓ Teach the student to introspect and analyze one's own listening errors.

✓ Teach the student to discriminate between fact and opinion.

✓ Teach the student to judge whether the speaker has accomplished his purpose.

Tool 68: Teaching Comprehension

Tool 69:
Multiple Intelligences

In 1983, Howard Gardner, a professor at Harvard University, introduced his theory of multiple intelligences (MI) in his book, *Frames of Mind: The Theory of Multiple Intelligences*. Using MI will allow students to learn in many ways and will help them understand their strengths, interests, and talents while, at the same time, offer them alternative avenues to share what they know.

Tips

Teachers: Study the multiple intelligences. Observe your students. Create a list of students in your class who exhibit these characteristics. As you present concepts and content material, allow students to demonstrate what they know through multiple intelligences. An understanding of your students and MI will be helpful as you design and use lesson plans, interdisciplinary units, alternative products, and assessments. Share with parents.

Parents: Parents also may study the characteristics, observe the child, share observations and questions with the teacher, and talk with the child about his strengths, interests, and talents and how he lets people know what he knows.

Multiple Intelligences

Verbal/Linguistic
✓ Thinks in words
✓ Is a good speaker
✓ Has highly developed vocabulary

Visual/Spatial
✓ Tends to think in pictures
✓ Uses mental images to retain information
✓ Learns and uses diagrams, maps, charts, pictures, videos, and hands-on projects

Logical/Mathematical
- ✓ Uses reason, logic, and numbers
- ✓ Thinks conceptually in logical and numerical patterns
- ✓ Likes to experiment

Bodily/Kinesthetic
- ✓ Controls body movements and handles objects skillfully
- ✓ Has good eye-hand coordination
- ✓ Learns through interacting with space around him or her

Musical/Rhythmic
- ✓ Appreciates music
- ✓ Produces music
- ✓ Thinks in sounds, rhythms, and patterns

Interpersonal
- ✓ Relates to others
- ✓ Understands others
- ✓ Sees things from other perspectives

Intrapersonal
- ✓ Uses self-reflection
- ✓ Is aware of own state of being
- ✓ Understands own feelings, relationships with others, and strengths and needs

Naturalist
- ✓ Understands his or her environment
- ✓ Applies science to own life
- ✓ Recognizes connection to nature

MI and Students

Verbal/Linguistic student(s): _____

_____

Visual/Spatial student(s): _____

_____

Logical/Mathematical student(s): _____

_____

Tool 69: Multiple Intelligences

Bodily/Kinesthetic student(s): _____

_____

Musical/Rhythmic student(s): _____

_____

Interpersonal student(s): _____

_____

Intrapersonal student(s): _____

_____

Naturalist student(s): _____

_____

Implications for instruction:

_____

_____

_____

_____

_____

_____

_____

_____

_____

_____

_____

Tool 69: Multiple Intelligences

Tool 70: Communication Template

Opening lines of communication between students and their teacher is essential.

Tips

Teachers: Make the following template available to students and explain its purpose and how students can deliver a note to you.

Communication Template

Dear _____,

I need some help with:

_____

_____

_____

_____

_____

_____

Please let me know when we could meet:

Date: _____ Time: _____

Place: _____

Thank you.

Tool 71:
Listening Skills

This tool demonstrates techniques for teaching, modeling, and practicing listening skills in and out of class.

Tips

Teachers and Parents: There is a difference between "hearing" and "listening." Listening requires attention and focus. With practice, this skill can improve!

Listening Skills

Concentrate!
✓ Focus on the speaker.
✓ Make eye contact.

Understand the Purpose!
✓ Identify what the speaker wants you to know.
✓ Think while listening about what the speaker is saying.
✓ Be positive and assume that you will learn something.

Take Notes!
✓ Record key words, main ideas, phrases, and details to keep you focused and on task.
✓ Jot down reminders to yourself.

Active Listening

Active listening is a process that allows you to hear and understand the message that is sent from someone else to you. It is an important skill when interacting with others. It is an especially powerful tool for conflict resolution. The process is as follows:
✓ Make eye contact.
✓ Acknowledge what is said.
✓ Paraphrase back to the speaker the content of the message.
✓ Confirm the message that is being sent.

Tool 72:
Evaluation Checklist

This checklist will assist you in gathering information about a student's academic skills.

Tips

Teachers and Parents: Teachers, parents, and students may use the following checklist as an evaluation tool.

Evaluation Checklist

Rate each statement according to the following scale:

1 = Never   2 = Sometimes   3 = Often   4 = Always

_____   Student works independently.

_____   Student shows motivation and tenacity when presented with activities commensurate with his or her ability.

_____   Student uses a variety of opportunities to show what he or she knows.

_____   Student is attentive.

_____   Student uses organizational skills.

_____   Student uses time management skills.

_____   Student uses technological tools.

_____   Student uses research skills.

_____   Student uses problem-solving skills.

_____   Student engages in activities that require more than just factual recall of information.

_____   Student uses a variety of materials and resources.

_____   Student makes connections in and across subject areas.

_____   Student seeks help when needed.

_____   Student functions well in a variety of working groups.

_____   Student shows consideration for others.

chapter 7

School Observations

Prior to the opening of the new school year, Ms. Smith joined her colleagues at a professional development meeting to review information about her incoming fifth-grade students. She was joined by her grade-level team, the school counselor, and the speech and language therapist. Ms. Smith had already received the index cards prepared by the students' previous year's teacher with the important academic, medical, social, and behavioral notes on each student. A roundtable discussion ensued regarding the strengths and needs of each student and the programs and services that would be provided. In addition, Ms. Smith rounded out the picture of each student by reviewing the cumulative records and the confidential records of children with disabilities. She and the school counselor had already met with the parents of children with disabilities during the August teacher preparation week.

G AT H E R I N G data about a child is imperative. The more a teacher knows and understands about a student, the better able she is to plan, prepare, and practice strategies that will work best for each student. Written records and staff input, including that from teachers in the arts and specialists, help to create a more complete student profile. In this respect it is very important to accurately keep and maintain records. Index cards are helpful for doing so, and teachers should be prepared to document the strengths and needs of their students, especially those with ADHD and other disabilities. Such documentation only aides future teachers in providing accommodations students need. Parents also should maintain orderly and accurate records, keeping copies of letters and other materials (including report cards and progress reports) sent home. By law, parents are eligible to receive copies of student records held by school districts. Parents may wish to periodically request copies of student records for their personal files. If the educator does not have accurate information from the student's previous teachers, he or she may wish to contact the parents, advocate, or case manager to learn as much about a child as possible (Silverman et al., 2009).

Tool 73:
Tracking ADHD Symptoms

There are many systems of observation. The idea is to really get a good sample of the child's current functioning. This tracking system demonstrates one method that parents and teachers can use to track a student's ADHD symptoms.

Tips

Teachers and Parents: Sometimes, overly formal observation systems miss the forest for the trees and fail to capture the primary functioning dynamics of the child in the school setting.

Tracking ADHD Symptoms

✓ Some observations can be effective in a very brief period of time (15 minutes) if the target behaviors are clear, small in number, and easily defined.

✓ An observation of 30 to 60 minutes is generally an optimum time frame.

✓ Sometimes, several short observations in school (or at home) are helpful. Observations in multiple subjects often are better, because each school subject has different, and often critically informative, task demands.

✓ For social skills observations, recess, the hallways, the cafeteria, the gymnasium, and line-ups might be best, while concentration might be better measured during a silent project.

✓ In some observations a checklist of no more than three to five target behaviors might be used if they are critical to the child's success and to the IEP or 504 plan, for example. A counting method such as instances per every 10 minutes might be helpful.

✓ Sometimes it is wise to use multiple observations at unpredictable times and settings when looking for a stable, generalized behavior of the child.

✓ Generally, if a person from outside the school, such as an advocate or psychologist, is observing, the child should not know that he or she is the target of the observation (although children often can sense when they are being observed). A psychologist who has already tested the child might send someone else into the setting to do the observation to avoid the examiner/student relationship affecting the observation.

✓ There are specific instances in which the child should know that a particular skill is being observed where the observer might, for instance, sit next to the child while the child works at a desktop assignment.

✓ Teachers should be sensitive to requirements of the observation, and the observer's job is to be clear about the requirements ahead of time.

✓ Time sampling observations are vital if a particular behavior is important at a given time of the day. For example, this would be implemented when looking for effectiveness or changes in medication effects or a reported behavior that only occurs in one class.

✓ When reporting ADHD symptoms for physician feedback on medications, use target core symptoms that the medication is designed to address such as: distractibility, restlessness, impulsivity, compliance, forgetfulness, organizational skills, depressed mood, anxiety, and so on. Use a limited number of clear behaviors.

✓ The "magic number seven" is important in describing rated behaviors on scales. For example, behavioral severity can be circled on a line with the numbers 1 through 7, with 1 being a very low amount, 4 in the middle, and 7 in the extreme. Raters do not function accurately and reliably with a much larger number of choice points. The best rating scales have 5 to 7 points.

Tool 73: Tracking ADHD Symptoms

Tool 74:
Functional Behavior
Assessment

When a child's behavior becomes a significant concern in school, whether or not a disability has been identified, school staff can specify the target behaviors and their antecedents and consequences to develop a plan of action. The assessment of the chain of events is called a functional behavior assessment (FBA) and a resultant plan is called a behavior intervention plan (BIP). Often the problematic behaviors are related to a disability that has already been identified and are the focal point of treatment and management of the disability. This is particularly true of students who have been classified with an emotional disturbance.

When educators have concerns about the behavior of a student with a disability, they are required by IDEA to undertake the functional behavior assessment process in order to determine why the student displays the behavior. Educational staff can then develop interventions to help the student display more appropriate behaviors.

Under IDEA 2004, educators must conduct an FBA when persistent behavioral concerns exist; they also are required by law to conduct it within 10 days of any singular offense by a student with a disability that is punishable by suspension or removal to an interim educational setting.

The FBA is the process of gathering and analyzing information about the student's behavior and accompanying circumstances in order to determine the purpose or intent of the actions.

The FBA was designed to:

✓ determine the appropriateness of educational placement and services,
✓ identify positive interventions to reduce the undesirable behavior, and
✓ select appropriate behaviors to be substituted in replacement of the inappropriate ones.

The FBA is based upon the following assumptions:

✓ challenging behaviors do not occur in isolation;
✓ behaviors occur in response to an identifiable stimulus;
✓ behaviors are governed by the consequences that follow them;
✓ behavior is a form of communication;
✓ misbehavior may be adaptive in some circumstances; and
✓ behaviors have a purpose, often:
  ▪ to get something (e.g., attention, money, good grades), or
  ▪ to avoid/escape something (e.g., punishment, embarrassment).

Tips

Teachers: It often is helpful to specifically identify the function of a child's behavior. It is important to not jump to conclusions without carefully analyzing the situation.

Functional Behavior Assessment (FBA)

Although an FBA might be spelled out in great detail according to the specific instructions contained in the format for each school jurisdiction, the teacher and parent should have the exact requirements very clearly listed.

- ✓ An FBA should have no more than three to five target behaviors.
- ✓ An FBA should avoid "psychologizing" about the causes of the behavior with unsubstantiated theories.
- ✓ On the other hand, an FBA should try to find identifiable predecessors or triggers for behavior.
- ✓ An FBA works best when educators, parents, and students take ownership for the behavior change, especially if the student identifies his or her own triggers.
- ✓ Positive, identifiable consequences will make the behavior plan truly a behavior modification plan and not just an empty exercise.

Tool 75:
Teacher Observations About Students on Medication

Teachers often are given permission by parents to work with pediatricians, psychologists, and psychiatrists as part of the monitoring process for students on medications.

Tips

Teachers: The following form may be helpful in gathering data to be shared with medical personnel.

Teacher Observations About Students on Medication

Name of Student: _____ Date: _____

Name of Medication: _____

Administration of Medication: _____

Notes:
- ❑ Behavior Problems Observed: _____

  _____

- ❑ Behavior Improvement Observed: _____

  _____

- ❑ Academic Impact Observed: _____

  _____

- ❑ Academic Improvement Observed: _____

  _____

Comments:

_____

_____

_____

_____

Tool 75: Teacher Observations About Students on Medication

chapter 8

Preparing for Meetings

A S teachers study a student's profile and work with other professionals, individualized intervention plans are developed that reflect the appropriate adaptations, modifications, and accommodations needed for that specific child.

Students who are determined to have learning disabilities may qualify for an Individualized Education Program (IEP). Part of the eligibility determination is based on a decision regarding whether or not the student requires specially designed instruction to meet the unique needs resulting from his or her disability. When it is decided that the student has a disability and needs special instruction, an IEP is developed. The IEP includes goals and objectives and provides a specific plan for direct instruction as needed. The IEP also includes classroom and testing accommodations (Weinfeld et al., 2006). The categories on an IEP form provide a structure for data collection and instructional implications. Categories include:

✓ Student and School Information
✓ Evaluation Eligibility Data
  ▪ Present Level of Functional Performance
  ▪ Health
  ▪ Physical
  ▪ Behavior
  ▪ Academic achievement
  ▪ Communication
  ▪ Assistive technology

✓ Service Provider
✓ Instructional and Testing Accommodations
  ▪ Timing
  ▪ Scheduling
  ▪ Setting

✓ Supplemental Aids, Services, Program Modification, and Supports
✓ Postsecondary Goals
✓ Course of Study
✓ Transition Services/Activities
✓ Student Accountability for General Curriculum

Not all students with attentional issues have an IEP. An alternative is the development of a 504 Plan. Like an IEP, a 504 Plan is a result of federal law, and can put into place formal accommodations to be used both in the classroom and in testing situations. Unlike an IEP, 504 Plans do not typically provide for special education instruction of any kind. They are administered and monitored by the "general" educators in the school, typically the guidance counselor (Weinfeld et al., 2006). Realistically, some children with attentional issues do not have either an IEP or a 504 plan, but need adaptations and accommodations. It therefore is imperative that teachers know their students' strengths and needs, and the strategies necessary to support a child in the classroom whether there is a formal document or not (Silverman et al., 2009).

Middle School and High School

Middle school and high school may be difficult for any student. For many kids with ADHD, the secondary experience may be more than difficult; it may be totally overwhelming. Students with ADHD often face the following challenges:
✓ academic intensity;
✓ hormonal changes;
✓ social issues;
✓ peer relationships;
✓ peer teasing, bullying, and rejection;
✓ establishing relationships with opposite sex;
✓ experimenting with illegal substances; and
✓ driving safely.

According to middle and high school teachers across the country, the adolescent with ADHD also may be faced with the following issues (Dendy, 2000, 2006; Dendy & Zeigler, 2003):

✓ completing and submitting homework on time,
✓ forgetting homework assignments,
✓ disorganization,
✓ motivation and persistence,
✓ specific academic challenges,
✓ planning ahead,
✓ disruptive behavior,
✓ issues with following directions,
✓ difficulty understanding expectations, and
✓ executive functioning deficits.

When Sammy completed his elementary school years and entered middle and high school, his attentional issues still needed to be addressed. However, the strategies he learned and his growing ability to be a self-advocate made his transition to secondary education less problematic.

Sammy had internalized the strategies that worked for him. These included:
✓ *preferential seating,*
✓ *task analysis of assignments,*
✓ *daily assignment notebook,*
✓ *use of highlighters for key words and concepts,*
✓ *social skills training learned with his counselor,*
✓ *use of assistive technology, and*
✓ *self-advocacy.*

Sammy, attending his own IEP meeting with his parents and school staff, created a plan to be utilized in his new school setting. The plan included continuing strategies that Sammy found successful and other strategies, such as:
✓ *working with his teachers on cues for attention,*
✓ *permission to move freely in the classroom when necessary,*
✓ *choice for alternative products and hands-on activities,*
✓ *unobtrusive assignment notebook check,*
✓ *periodic student/teacher conferencing, and*
✓ *interim checks on long-term assignments.*

Sammy's parents created an action plan with Sammy and the staff. Recognizing that Sammy was responsible for his learning and also recognizing the importance of the possible negative effects of providing excessive or unnecessary accommodations, the need to select accommodations based on the impact of the individual student's disability, the need to move students from dependence to independence, and the need to evaluate and revise adaptations and accommodations, Sammy and the school team chose the relevant interventions and built in a periodic evaluation on his progress. Appropriate changes would occur to make sure that Sammy was a successful learner (Weinfeld et al., 2006).

Sammy had already learned skills in landscape design from his architect mentor. He was a regular helper in leading students to beautify his elementary school and led a part-time work team mowing lawns in his neighborhood and improving landscaping with the help of a landscape designer identified by his mentor.

Other Student Profiles

Sammy is one profile of a child with attentional issues. He is a model success story, where everything has gone right, because of informed and conscious planning. Although the best practices listed work with all children, the specifics will be vastly different from one child to another. For example, Sammy does not exhibit major behavior problems that some students show in the school setting. If Sammy had challenging behaviors, the teacher would include strategies to address them. DuPaul and Stoner (2002) offer excellent guidance for interventions that address academic behavior problems, including using more than one intervention strategy, combining proactive and reactive strategies to prevent and manage problem behaviors, individualizing interventions, and implementing strategies close to the time and place that specific behaviors occur.

Tool 76:
IEP and 504 Plan Meetings

The following tool is helpful for parents in collaborating with the school at IEP and 504 Plan meetings.

Tips

Parents: ADHD is recognized as a disorder under IDEA. The following checklists may be helpful to use when attending IEP or 504 Plan meetings.

IEP and 504 Plan Meetings

A child should receive an IEP or 504 Plan if the following occur:
- ❏ Child is diagnosed with ADHD and the diagnosis is recognized by the school.
- ❏ Child's ADHD results in an adverse effect on educational performance.
- ❏ Appropriate information has been considered in determining adverse school performance.
- ❏ Special education services are offered or are not offered.

Writing IEP and 504 Plans
- ❏ Research appropriate information regarding your child's strengths and needs, adaptations and accommodations, and programs and services available.
- ❏ Record and bring essential information about the child to meetings regarding findings and recommendations from evaluations.
- ❏ Create a wish list of appropriate programs and services.
- ❏ Work collaboratively—do not become adversarial.
- ❏ Document the recommendations and decisions made at the meeting.
- ❏ Bring someone to the meeting with you if possible: an expert, family member, or friend.
- ❏ Participate fully in the meeting, including asking questions.
- ❏ Make sure the roles and responsibilities for delivering services are clearly stated and recorded.
- ❏ Include attention to all aspects of the child: academic, social, emotional, and behavioral.
- ❏ Get and keep copies of documents and records.
- ❏ Get help if needed from CHADD, an advocate, or another party.

Tool 77:
IEP and 504 Plans Checklist

The following checklist helps parents with the process of preparing for and attending school IEP meetings and 504 Plan meetings.

Tips

Parents: This checklist will get you prepared to be an effective advocate for you child at IEP meetings and Section 504 Plan meetings.

IEP and 504 Plans Checklist

❏ **Do your homework:** Learn as much as possible about how your child is functioning and what your child needs. If your child was evaluated privately, make sure you thoroughly comprehend the findings and that the recommendations are relevant to your child's school. If your child was evaluated by the school district, make sure to get a copy of the results and try to discuss them with the evaluator before the meeting to avoid any surprises and to make sure you thoroughly understand the results.

❏ **Do more homework:** Prior to the first meeting, make sure you are familiar with the differences between IDEA for special education services eligibility, and eligibility for accommodations under Section 504.

❏ **Do even more homework:** Try to learn as much as you can about the accommodations and services your child needs and determine which of these are available at your child's school. It is easier to be an effective advocate for your child if you know what you are advocating for. Goals and objectives on IEPs and 504 Plans must be relevant to your child, realistic, and measurable.

❏ **Be prepared:** Make sure you come to the meeting with a clear understanding of the purpose of the meeting, who will be in attendance, and what is going to happened during the meeting. It is your right to receive a written invitation prior to the meeting, know who is going to present, and why it has been called.

❏ **Bring your wish list:** Be proactive. Make sure that you do not have to just react to the proposal made by the school. Instead, come with your own ideas based on your very important knowledge of your child and the school.

❏ **Make sure that all promises discussed in the meeting are documented in the written plan:** It is very important that all services, accommodations, and modifications discussed in the meeting are written down in a formal plan. If these changes are not written down, they cannot be enforced.

❏ **Bring your spouse, a relative, or a friend:** Parents often find it valuable to have someone there to support them, be another good listener, and take good notes, so that you are available to participate more actively in the meeting.

❏ **Bring your independent expert:** When possible, it often is beneficial to have your private diagnostician or therapist participate in the meetings.

❏ **Know you have the right to ask questions:** Don't be afraid to ask questions to clarify anything or get more information. It is your right to participate in the meeting fully or to request that the meeting is reconvened on another day to allow for further discussion.

❏ **The devil is in the specific details:** It is important that the plan identifies who will be responsible for making sure that each aspect of the plan is being implemented, when the change will be implemented, and how the changes will be monitored and evaluated. Ask to create an information feedback loop to keep you informed of your child's progress at school on a regular basis to know how the plan is working.

❏ **Manage behavior problems:** If your child is struggling with behavioral problems at school, make sure the plan includes a behavior management plan to address the child's difficulties through positive reinforcement. It may be helpful to request having a functional behavioral assessment to get a better understanding of the behavior.

❏ **Know that Other Health Impairment (OHI) is an option:** Many schools will only consider students with the diagnosis of ADHD for eligibility for accommodations under Section 504. However, eligibility for an IEP and special education under the Other Health Impaired category is another viable option depending on the specific needs and functioning of your child.

❏ **Get and keep organized records:** It is important to get copies of the reports from IEP and 504 Plan meetings. Create a file with all of your child's report cards, reports from meetings, correspondences, and behavioral or disciplinary records. You may find that you will need them later on.

❏ **When possible, use a peaceful approach:** It is likely that everyone will lose in adversarial meetings. Try to work collaboratively with the staff at your child's school as much as possible. Take an assertive role as an advocate for your child, but not an aggressive stance. Make sure

Tool 77: IEP and 504 Plans Checklist

to give the school staff positive recognition for the efforts they have made with your child. Avoid blaming the school or making it personal if there is a problem. If disputes or conflicts arise, try to mediate, compromise, or come up with a creative solution whenever possible.

❑ **If needed, get help:** If a problem arises in a meeting and your having difficulty resolving it, seek help through an advocate in your area or get legal advice. CHADD can be helpful in connecting you with professionals in your area.

Note. Adapted from Harman (2001).

Tool 78:
Intervention Plan

This tool assists teachers in developing appropriate, individualized plans for each specific student's needs.

Tips

Teachers: Use this tool to analyze what is currently in place for the student and to make a plan of what could be done.

Intervention Plan

Name:

Date:

School:

A. Evidence of Gifts:

Test scores:

Performance in school:
(When does the student show interest, perseverance, self-regulation, and outstanding achievement?)

Performance in the community:

Evidence of Learning Difficulties:
(reading, writing, organization, memory, specific learning disabilities, ADHD)

Test scores:

Performance in school:

Behavioral/Attentional Problems:

Performance in school:

Performance at home:

B. Current Program:

Gifted instruction:

Adaptations:

Accommodations:

Special instruction:

Behavior/attention management:
(Plans, medication)

Tool 78: Intervention Plan

Counseling:
(In-school, therapy)

Case management:
(Home to school communication; communication among staff)

C. Recommendations

Gifted instruction:

Adaptations:

Accommodations:

Special instruction:

Behavior/attention management:

Case management:

D. Next Steps:

Tool 79:
Teacher Conferences

This tool assists teachers in preparing for and holding teacher conferences.

Tips

Teachers: Being familiar with the following guidelines will help you in holding productive teacher conferences.

Teacher Conferences

Preparation

- ✓ Prepare the main points in advance by writing them down.
- ✓ Rehearse your presentation.
- ✓ Be aware of your dress and appearance with parents.
- ✓ Don't mention a problem without a solution, preferably a best practices solution.
- ✓ Do not let problems build up without contacting parents. Don't spring big surprises on parents they should have known about earlier.
- ✓ Invite both parents if there are two. Two separate conferences may be necessary when parents are estranged and actively adversarial with each other.
- ✓ Beware of legal timelines.

The Teacher's Impression on the Parents

- ✓ Do not use first names. It is overly familiar and impedes separation for doing business. Don't try to be a friend. A first name might be permissible in a very small town where calling someone Ms. X would be silly if she is your neighbor.
- ✓ Many parents come to the parent/teacher conference with their own anxieties as well as the ones they bring about their child. Some parents of children with disabilities had and have their own issues. There often are feelings of trepidation upon entering a school. Understand that everyone isn't school oriented.
- ✓ Don't assume that Jennifer Smith's mother is Mrs. Smith. Get the names right. This won't be a problem if you have read the child's whole folder (recommended).

✓ Create an atmosphere of collaborative problem solving from the beginning. Visualize yourself as serving the parents, but you are not the parents' employee. They don't supervise you.

✓ Although the parent often is the second-most important consumer of our services, as the child's guardian, the parent is the gateway to the improved quality of life for the whole child.

✓ It is always about the child first. Always keep that in mind. When you are called upon to put your judgment on the line, keep the child in mind as your mission. No authority or committee should override your personal integrity and best-considered judgment.

✓ The greeting should be confident and positive. A good handshake is really important. Beware, however, that not all cultures use a handshake.

✓ Start and end with something positive about the child or your relationship with the child.

✓ Don't harp on weaknesses and failures even in the worse case. Keep the tone positive.

✓ Sometimes a little recent positive performance or humorous anecdote is a good start.

✓ You might refer to a student's paper, picture, or project displayed on the bulletin board.

✓ Commend a parent for his or her investment, involvement, and successes in raising a good citizen and/or a good achiever.

✓ The parent conference is more about the process than the content. But if you have no content, then you will not succeed. If you aren't prepared they know it, just like kids do.

✓ Be a really good active listener.

✓ Don't do home visits unless the administration knows and approves, and don't go alone.

✓ Do not engage in nonprofessional relationships with parents. Also, watch what is displayed on your Facebook and MySpace accounts.

✓ Invite but control volunteerism.

✓ Avoid talking about other children and comparisons to other children in the family.

✓ Refer complaints, especially about school personnel or policies, to the administration.

✓ Schedule adequate time for the meeting. Twenty to thirty minutes usually is adequate. If you're scheduling back-to-back conferences, be sure to allow enough time between them (10 minutes or so) so you can make necessary notes on the just-conducted conference and prepare for the upcoming one. Schedule 45 minutes to 2 hours for complicated IEP cases.

Tool 79: Teacher Conferences

✓ Be careful about permission to conduct the meeting and share information. Find out who has custody for educational purposes. Try not to be involved in custody disputes.

Conducting the Meeting

✓ Do not permit threats and offensive language to or about anyone in the meeting. Invite parents to use appropriate language for the school environment. If this suggestion does not work, invite the parents to leave.

✓ Always invite a witness when you fear you will be misunderstood or threatened.

✓ Don't meet with risky parents alone after school.

✓ Explain the agenda for the meeting.

✓ When you stick to IEP objectives you are dealing with something legal, born of consensus. It is not just your opinion. Focus on critical IEP objectives and not child rearing in general.

✓ Stick with data and not interpretation.

✓ Explain commonly used statistics. Use a chart or graph.

✓ Be careful about your professional jargon, including the name of tests and measurements that parents will not recognize.

✓ Try to explain test score distribution through standard scores using the normal curve. Be careful about the use of developmental ages or percentile ranks. Grade equivalents have some validity but need to be explained with care.

✓ Don't avoid or shy away from critical issues.

✓ Respect the parents' intuition. Often parents see things we do not. They have their children most of the day and weekends. You have a 6-hour view.

✓ You must report abuse if suspected, and you may have to tell parents that you reported them.

✓ Never push medication. You may suggest a physician's consultation.

✓ Do not try to be a counselor or social worker if you are a teacher. Refer them to one if necessary.

✓ Be strong and consistent about tardiness and absences. Children can lose private school funding through excessive absences and may not receive educational services of the same quality if funding is terminated.

✓ Know your school policies.

✓ Explain the goal or goals that you will be setting for the child in school. Make these goals attainable so that the child will meet with success. The parents must have the same goals at home.

Conclusion

✓ Summarize the conference. Thank and praise the parents for coming to the meeting. Thank them for their input and how you look forward to continue working with them. They should leave feeling comfortable about what just took place.

✓ Agree on a regular time and method for ongoing communication.

✓ Explain the next checkpoint.

✓ Refer parents to appropriate resources.

✓ Inform them about when to expect a written copy of documents.

Tool 79: Teacher Conferences

chapter 9

Communication Between Teachers, Parents, and Professionals

Sammy's parents and Ms. Smith communicate regularly throughout the school year. The daily assignment sheet is ongoing, as is a weekly progress report. They set up an e-mail correspondence when it is needed and parent/teacher conferences are held periodically to address Sammy's progress. Permission is received for Ms. Smith to be in contact, when necessary, with Sammy's doctors.

THE general educator keeps the lines of communication open between students, staff, and parents/guardians. When all parties work respectfully to establish open and direct communication, a lasting partnership is possible. Parents should not hesitate to contact their child's teacher with concerns and also should be willing to provide praise when they recognize that a teacher is working effectively with their child. The same goes for teachers: Parents need to know about both the problems, concerns, and worries regarding their child *and* the good things teachers see the child doing. Discussing the child's strengths or progress with parents in a positive manner can build student self-confidence, leading to more academic success (Silverman et al., 2009).

Tool 80:
School-Home Report Card

A helpful technique is to use a "report card" that is taken between home and school each day. This simple chart will make it easy to get feedback from the child's teacher about how the child did in the various target areas. As a result, parents are able to reward the child with privileges based on his or her behavior in school.

Tips

Teachers and Parents: The following guidelines are suggested for creating and implementing the home-school report card:

1. The child's teacher and parent should discuss the plan for the child. Working together is important because the teacher needs to fill out the ratings each day and it is helpful to create a collaborative relationship between the parents and the teacher from the beginning. Parents should discuss with the teacher a plan of trying to carefully monitor the child's behavior at school and at home. This system will give parents and teachers a lot of information without requiring a lot time.

2. Decide what target behaviors to include. Input from the parent and teacher is essential in the process. Determine the two or three key areas that the parent and the teacher think are the most important and where improvement is necessary. Some examples could include completing assigned class work, following class rules, treating peers with respect, and waiting your turn before talking.

3. Decide how to rate the child for each item. Each day the child's teacher and parent (for homework) will rate the child on the two to three key areas that were chosen in step two. Often parents and teachers like a simple one to five rating scale where 1 indicates a very poor job on the specified behavior, 3 indicates a satisfactory job, and 5 indicates a very good job.

4. Then construct the daily rating forms. The child's teacher and parent should have copies of this form so that he or she can complete them each day for the child to bring home.

5. Discuss the plan with the child. It is important that the child understands this plan and is on board with it. Explain that it will provide him or her the opportunity to earn extra rewards for doing a good job. It is extremely important that the child does not see it as a punishment. The expectations and rewards must be explained clearly from the start.

Additionally, it is helpful for the teacher to review the ratings each day with the child to make sure the child understands why he or she received the rating. Make sure the child knows what scores he or she needs to earn each day and the target behaviors to earn the agreed upon rewards.

School-Home Report Card

Student's Name: _____

Date: _____

Circle one number for each behavior below.

Remains on task during class work	1 2 3 4 5
Raises hand to participate	1 2 3 4 5
Comes to class prepared	1 2 3 4 5

Comments:

_____

_____

_____

_____

_____

Note: 1 = very poor; 2 = poor; 3 = satisfactory; 4 = good; 5 = very good

Tool 81:
Daily Communication Log

Effective communication between teachers and parents is extremely important to ensure the success of students with ADHD.

Tips

Teachers and Parents: A log similar to the one below should be hole punched and placed in the student's notebook. Both parents and teachers write comments to create an ongoing dialog about the student. Communication can include discussion about grades, improvements, concerns, missing assignments, behavior, and so on.

Daily Communication Log

DATE Week of ____	Parent Comments	Teacher Comments
Monday		
Tuesday		
Wednesday		
Thursday		
Friday		

Tool 82:
Report to Parents

As you gather pieces of information, use this form to summarize information in order to provide a clear understanding of an individual child's educational history, strengths, needs, and learning styles.

Tips

Teachers: Work with parents to complete the form. Share with responsible staff.

Report to Parents

Student name:_____

Review of student records, including the following:

Recommendations for additional needed information:

Analysis of child's strengths and needs based on record review:

Information about specific educational programs:

Additional resources and related services:

Short-term action plan:

Long-term action plan:

Persons responsible for action plans and services:

Follow-up:

Tool 83:
Parent-Teacher
Conference Guide

The following tool can be used to structure a meaningful conference.

Tips

Teachers: Effective and efficient parent-teacher conferences require planning. When time is at a premium, this is a useful instrument because it contains information about the "total child"—socially, emotionally, and intellectually. In addition, this guide can be shared with the student before the parent-teacher conference so that everyone is on the same page.

Parent-Teacher Conference Guide

Student Name: _____

Grade: _____   Date: _____

Areas in which student shows strength, growth, or has a need (S = strength; G = growth; N = need)

Intellectual

_____ Initiative
_____ Resourcefulness
_____ Problem solving
_____ Follow through on plans
_____ Evaluates own work
_____ Originality

Social

_____ Cooperation with teacher
_____ Cooperation with other students
_____ Self-reliant
_____ Leadership among peers
_____ Ability to follow

_____ Ability to give and take
_____ Appreciation of others
_____ Contributes to group effort
_____ Responsibility

Emotional

_____ Self-control
_____ Speech and conduct
_____ Respect for rights and property of others
_____ Consideration toward others
_____ Recognition of standards
_____ Attentiveness

Work Habits

_____ Prompt
_____ Persistent
_____ Completes tasks commensurate with ability
_____ Follows directions
_____ Consideration of others while they are working
_____ Independent
_____ Achievement in relation to child's ability
_____ Achievement in relation to child's goal

Tool 84:
Identification Data
Gathering Tools

It is critical that multiple measures are used to help us find our kids with learning differences. These measures tap into verbal and nonverbal strengths, reading and math abilities, and other strengths that kids share through their talents and interests. This information should be gathered from parents, students, teachers, and community members who see kids from a variety of perspectives.

Tips

Teachers: Find out the specific tools that are available to you when identifying students. Work with appropriate staff members to collect data about this student population. Learn how the data impact instruction. Implement the appropriate strategies with students. Interpret the data to understand the instructional implications.

Parents: Find out the specific tools used by your school for identification purposes. When advocating for your child, ask questions regarding the tools that may be used for your child. Understand your rights within this process.

Identification Data Gathering Tools

Here are some examples of tools that can typically be used in identifying students with learning differences:

❏ **Subjective and Objective Information:**
- Verbal and nonverbal test data
- Teacher and parent checklists
- Portfolios/work samples

❏ **Formal Data** (These tests are given by way of example rather than as definitive because individual instruments can change over time.):
- Achievement tests (California, Iowa)
- Aptitude/ability tests
- Nonverbal reasoning tests (Naglieri Test of Nonverbal Reasoning, Raven—Standard Progressive Matrices)
- Educational assessments (Woodcock Johnson, WIAT)
- Psychological assessments (WISC-IV, Stanford-Binet)

- Connor's Scales (Attention)
- Teacher checklists (Renzulli Hartman Behavioral Rating Scale)
- Teacher and parent rating scales (SIGS)

❑ **Informal Data:**
- Nominations from parents, staff
- Portfolios/work samples
- Teacher observations
- Preassessment data

❑ **Nontraditional Data:**
- Community nomination
- Interview
- Peer nomination
- Student nomination

❑ **Potential Charts:**
- ORR Charts

Tool 85:
Teacher and Parent Resources

It often can be difficult to know where to look for current and accurate information about ADHD. The following list provides websites and books where this information may be readily accessed.

Tips

Teachers and Parents: Use the following websites and other resources to gain up-to-date information on ADHD.

Teacher and Parent Resources

Websites

The National Institute of Mental Health—http://www.nimh.nih.gov

U.S. Department of Education Office of Special Education and Rehabilitative Services—http://www.ed.gov/about/offices/list/osers/index.html

Children and Adults with Attention-Deficit/Hyperactivity Disorder (CHADD)—http://www.chadd.org

Nemours—http://www.nemours.org

LD Online—http://www.ldonline.org

Attention Deficit Disorder Association (ADDA)—http://www.add.org

National Center for Learning Disabilities—http://www.ncld.org

Learning Disabilities Association of America—http://www.ldaamerica.org

All Kinds of Minds—http://www.allkindsofminds.org

The REACH Institute—http://www.thereachinstitute.org

Council for Exceptional Children—http://www.cec.sped.org

Smart Kids with Learning Disabilities—http://www.smartkidswithld.org

Wrightslaw Libraries—http://www.wrightslaw.com

National Dissemination Center for Children With Disabilities—http://www.nichcy.org

National Resource Center on AD/HD—http://www.help4adhd.org

Parent Encouragement Program—http://www.parentencouragement.org

GreatSchools—http://www.greatschools.net

Information on Attention Deficit Disorder & ADHD—http://www.helpforadd.com/info

Recording for the Blind & Dyslexic—http://www.rfbd.org

ADDitude Magazine ADHD at School—http://www.additudemag.com/adhd-guide/adhd-at-school.html

Books

Bain, L. J. (1991). *A parent's guide to attention deficit disorders.* New York, NY: Delta.

Barkley, R. A. (1991). *Attention-deficit hyperactivity disorder: A clinical workbook.* New York, NY: Guilford.

Barkley, R. A. (2000). *Taking charge of ADHD: The complete, authoritative guide for parents.* New York, NY: Guilford.

Bramer, J. S. (1996). *Succeeding in college with attention deficit disorders.* Plantation, FL: Specialty Press.

Caffrey, J. A. (1997). *First star I see.* Fairport, NY: Verbal Images.

Coloroso, B. (1994). *Kids are worth it!* Toronto, ON: Somerville House.

DuPaul, G. H., & Stoner, G. (1994). *ADHD in the school: Assessment and intervention strategies.* New York, NY: Guilford.

Fowler, M. C. (1990). *Maybe you know my kid: A parent's guide to identifying, understanding and helping your child with ADHD.* New York, NY: Birch Lane.

Galvin, M. (1995). *Otto learns about his medicine: A story about medicine for children with ADHD.* Washington, DC: Magination Press.

Gantos, J. (2000). *Joey Pigza loses control.* New York, NY: Farrar, Straus & Giroux.

Gehret, J. (1991). *Eagle eyes: A child's guide to paying attention* (2nd ed.). Fairport, NY: Verbal Images Press.

Goldstein, S. G. (1995). *Understanding and managing children's classroom behavior.* New York, NY: Wiley.

Goldstein, S., & Goldstein, M. (1993). *Hyperactivity: Why won't my child pay attention? A complete guide to ADD for parents, teachers, and community agencies.* New York, NY: Wiley.

Hallowell, E. M., & Ratey, J. J. (1994). *Driven to distraction: Recognizing and coping with attention deficit disorder from childhood to adulthood.* New York, NY: Pantheon.

Janover, C. (1997). *Zipper, the kid with ADHD.* Bethesda, MD: Woodbine House.

Jensen, P. S. (2005). *Making the system work for your child with ADHD.* New York, NY: Guilford.

Nadeau, K., Littman, E., & Quinn, P. (2000). *Understanding girls with AD/HD.* Silver Spring, MD: Advantage Books.

Nadeau, K. G., & Dixon, E. B. (1991). *Learning to slow down and pay attention.* Annandale, VA: Chesapeake Psychological Publications.

Nadeau, K. G., Dixon, E. B., & Biggs, S. (1993). *School strategies for ADD teens.* Annandale, VA: Chesapeake Psychological Publications.

Nemiroff, M. A., & Annunziata, J. (1998). *Help is on the way: A child's book about ADD.* Washington, DC: Magination Press.

Parker, H. C. (1992). *ADAPT teacher planbook.* Plantation, FL: Impact.

Parker, R. N. (1992). *Making the grade: An adolescent's struggle with ADD.* Plantation, FL: Impact.

Quinn, P. (1991). *Putting on the brakes: A child's guide to understanding and gaining control over attention deficit hyperactivity disorder* (ADHD). New York, NY: Magination Press.

Silverman, S. M., Iseman, J. S., & Jeweler, S. (2009). *School success for kids with ADHD.* Waco, TX: Prufrock Press.

Smith, M. (1997). *Pay attention, Slosh!* Morton Grove, IL: Albert Whitman.

Weiss, G., & Hechtman, L. T. (1994). *Hyperactive children grown up* (2nd ed.). New York, NY: Guilford.

Zimmert, D. (2001). *Eddie enough!* Bethesda, MD: Woodbine House.

Tool 85: Teacher and Parent Resources

Tool 86:
Collaborating With the
Student's Pediatrician

This tool provides information about how the school can work collaboratively with pediatricians.

Tips

Teachers: Assign one person to be the case manager to speak with the pediatrician. Often, this is the school nurse or counselor.

Collaborating With the
Student's Pediatrician

✓ Be sure that confidentiality statements have been signed to communicate with the pediatrician.
✓ Identify yourself and attempt to establish a form of communication convenient to both parties.
✓ Identify a few primary target behaviors affected by medication to discuss, especially if they are 504 Plan or IEP targets.
✓ Be consistent in focusing on those targets when discussing the student.
✓ Try to be objective in describing any changes or no change in specific behaviors.

Tool 87:
Collaborating With the Student's Mental Health Therapist

This tool provides information about how the school can work collaboratively with mental health therapists.

Tips

Teachers: Assign one person to be the case manager to speak with the mental health therapist. Often, this is the school nurse or counselor.

Collaborating With the Student's Mental Health Therapist

✓ Be sure that confidentiality statements have been signed to communicate with the mental health therapist.
✓ Identify yourself and attempt to establish a form of communication convenient to both parties.
✓ Identify a few primary target behaviors to discuss and monitor, especially if they are 504 Plan or IEP targets.
✓ Try to develop a universal language of terms to use with the therapist, parents, educational team, and child.
✓ Identify mutual community resources of support or potential support to the student.
✓ Try not to practice psychoanalysis yourself. Leave the internal dynamics to the professionals. Focus on observable and relevant behaviors.

chapter 10

Tools for Parents

TEACHERS and parents are most effective when they work together as partners in the learning process for children with ADHD. The following information may prove helpful to educators in understanding a comprehensive plan for parents as they work with their child.

Jack struggles in school, especially in completing assignments on time. His teachers frequently comment that he seems bright, but also note that he is distracted easily and that he often needs reminders to stay focused on his class work. Jack is a daydreamer who looks out the window or wanders around the classroom. He often gets in trouble for calling out or talking during lessons. At home, Jack's behavior is quite similar. His parents note that he easily forgets what he is supposed to be doing and has trouble getting up in the morning and going to bed at night. He loses things like toys and games, gets in trouble for climbing on the couch, and can't sit still at the dinner table. Jack has difficulty making and keeping friends. His peers often complain that he interrupts them and won't take turns.

Jack recently was diagnosed with ADHD. His parents worry that his disorder may never allow him to receive the education he needs and deserves.

The following suggestions will help any parent whose child with ADHD struggles in school (Silverman et al., 2009):

    1. **Obtain accurate diagnosis of your child's problems.** Many parents initially are confused about the diagnosis of ADHD. Often they

seek or are led to medication before the condition is clearly identified properly. Be aware that other conditions and medical issues frequently resemble ADHD and should be ruled out by professionals. Parents often find it helpful to speak first with their child's pediatrician or family doctor about their concerns. Although some pediatricians may complete an assessment themselves, they often refer families to a mental health specialist whom they know and trust. During the evaluation, you should share any relevant information that may help the clinician accurately understand your child's developmental history. It frequently is beneficial to share the information that is gained through the evaluation with your child's teachers.

2. **Identify and nurture your child's strengths.** Love and acceptance is key here. Emphasize your child's strengths and interests, setting a positive tone that incorporates what he does well into his daily challenges. Ask any adult working with your child to always keep these strengths in mind. Often, by the time the child is identified, he already is seen as a "problem." Children with ADHD tend to incorporate these viewpoints, creating a negative self-image, which can lead to their seeking attention through negative behaviors. A positive view of the child for himself and for his significant others needs to be jump-started early in the game to begin turning around the negative view the child has established in his mind and the minds of others. Praise and emphasis on improvement can help increase a child's self-esteem.

3. **Educate yourself.** Read books, watch films, join organizations, and attend lectures, seminars, or parent training programs. Myth busting is very important, especially as more and more confusing and misleading information exists throughout the media and websites. Many parents find that parent education and support groups help with the initial acceptance of the diagnosis and provide strategies for helping their children manage their symptoms of ADHD. The resource box we've provided includes many reputable web resources for parent education.

4. **Consider counseling.** Parent training and counseling on child behavior management is available, usually through centers or mental health practitioners. In these sessions, an attempt is made to maximize consistency between parents in philosophy and techniques of child rearing. Parents who agree on how to manage a child's negative behaviors (and put their decisions into action) create an environment of safe discipline, security, love, and acceptance. A sense of teamwork and good communication is essential to being successful parents in any situation.

5. **Manage your stress.** As parents, we know that parenting any child isn't easy. It can be filled with times of great joy. But there are, of course, times that challenge us as we work with our kids. In particular, parenting a child or adolescent with ADHD can be frustrating and exhausting. In order to effectively manage a child's condition, it is important to feel prepared by accessing information that will support the child and help her acquire the appropriate services to address the disorder. In addition, you need to identify symptoms of your own stress. Strive to be a calm island in the life of your child, who is experiencing disruption in her own nervous system.

6. **Carefully monitor medications.** Prescription drugs are touchy subjects for many parents. However, research clearly has demonstrated that medication can be the most effective intervention for some children with ADHD. Typically, medication is prescribed by pediatricians or child psychiatrists. When medications are prescribed, they should be fully explained along with a discussion of possible side effects. We are at a time when the public, especially parents and professionals, is very confused about the effectiveness and safety of medications. Exaggerated stories of side effects and the lethality of medications abound. Although parents may fear incorporating medication into their child's daily routine, in order for this treatment to be successful all parties must be "on board." Thus, you should raise any questions or concerns about the medication to your child's doctor, but you also should follow through to make sure your child is taking the medication as prescribed. If you continue to have concerns about the medication, consider getting a second opinion. However, you should never stop or start a medication without the approval of a medical professional.

7. **Emphasize good nutrition.** A hungry child can be an inattentive, depressed, and angry child. Hunger can be due to poor nutrition as much as it can be due to low volumes of food. A balanced, healthy diet is a requisite for development and learning. We are not suggesting that poor diet alone always engenders ADHD symptoms, but poor diet can be part of a lifestyle of too much passive entertainment, lack of recreation, and inadequate supervision or structure.

8. **Put someone in charge.** Assign a responsible adult (either a parent, therapist, school counselor, special educator, or school nurse) to communicate with all relevant parties regarding medications and preplanned intervention strategies.

9. **Make sure your child receives help in school**. Federal law requires that children diagnosed as having special needs receive specific plans of action to improve their educations, called Individualized Education Programs (IEPs). Upon diagnosis, a plan for your child's

education should be developed in conjunction with his school staff that includes classroom accommodations or special education services. Children with ADHD rarely find themselves actively engaged in instruction to the same degree as children without the disorder. Teaching strategies must take into account management, class environment factors, teaching techniques, and specific instructional strategies appropriate for the child.

10. **Negotiate a contract between home and school**. Write a contract focusing on appropriate behavior and improvement at home and school. This can be taken between home and school each day, perhaps in a daily planner. In collaboration with the teacher, identify class work, homework, and organizational skill objectives for each subject. Monitor compliance with these objectives through periodic teacher and parent ratings of attention, activity level, and related personality/behavior variables. Such consistency in expectation only creates a more secure and dependable environment for your child.

11. **Build your child's self-esteem through counseling.** Individual and/or group counseling for your child should focus on self-evaluation, self-monitoring, and educational self-advocacy. It also should address issues related to peer relations and self-esteem. Group counseling or therapy will not cure or even alleviate the core symptoms of ADHD. However, there are many aspects of a child's development and mental health that may be improved through therapy, particularly in regard to self-esteem, leading to a happier overall outlook and more positive behavior.

12. **Manage your child's stress**. Explore calming and relaxation techniques to teach your child how to experience, nurture, and monitor calmness and peacefulness. Many children with ADHD have no experience of feeling calm or being at peace. Calming exercises like meditation may be valuable techniques that might be incorporated into life as children develop. Exercises like yoga can improve self-control, which can help children learn to focus their attention better in other tasks, including schoolwork.

Tool 88:
A 12-Point Multimodal Treatment Plan for Children and Adolescents With ADHD Annotated Checklist

It is our belief that interventions are effective and most powerful when they occur early and are integrated and systematic. We believe we have isolated practical interventions that can be conceptualized in 12 components. Take note: This is not a "12-step" program. ADHD is *not* an addiction. The steps are not always sequential or numbered, and they are not all necessary for each child. This plan also is not a "decision tree." The components represent a menu of broad options that can be combined to create helpful solutions. They are to be increasingly based on research as solid studies are brought forward and used artfully based on solid training, experience, and judgment. In a collaborative program where interventions are carefully selected, everyone wins, especially the child (Silverman et al., 2009).

Tips

Parents: In the opener for Chapter 10, "Tools for Parents," you will find explanations for each of the 12-points. On the checklist, put a check next to the suggestions you have taken and record the additional appropriate information. Steps Taken: Record what you have done to complete the task. Notes: Write down information that you have gathered related to the task. Next Steps: List what you plan to do. If you have not checked some of the 12-points, consider how the suggestion may be beneficial to you and your child.

A 12-Point Multimodal Treatment Plan for Children and Adolescents With ADHD Annotated Checklist

❏   1. Obtain accurate diagnosis of your child's problems.

- ▪   Steps Taken: _____

   _____

- ▪   Notes: _____

   _____

- ▪   Next Steps: _____

   _____

❏   2. Identify and nurture your child's strengths.

- ▪   Steps Taken: _____

   _____

- ▪   Notes: _____

   _____

- ▪   Next Steps: _____

   _____

❏   3. Educate yourself.

- ▪   Steps Taken: _____

   _____

- ▪   Notes: _____

   _____

- ▪   Next Steps: _____

❏   4. Consider counseling.

- ▪ Steps Taken: _____

  _____

- ▪ Notes: _____

  _____

- ▪ Next Steps: _____

  _____

❏   5. Manage your stress.

- ▪ Steps Taken: _____

  _____

- ▪ Notes: _____

  _____

- ▪ Next Steps: _____

  _____

❏   6. Carefully monitor medications.

- ▪ Steps Taken: _____

  _____

- ▪ Notes: _____

  _____

- ▪ Next Steps: _____

  _____

❏   7. Emphasize good nutrition.

- ▪ Steps Taken: _____

  _____

Tool 88: A 12-Point Multimodal Treatment Plan

- ▪ Notes: _____

  _____

- ▪ Next Steps: _____

  _____

❑ 8. Put someone in charge.

- ▪ Steps Taken: _____

  _____

- ▪ Notes: _____

  _____

- ▪ Next Steps: _____

  _____

❑ 9. Make sure your child receives help in school.

- ▪ Steps Taken: _____

  _____

- ▪ Notes: _____

  _____

- ▪ Next Steps: _____

  _____

❑ 10. Negotiate a contract between home and school.

- ▪ Steps Taken: _____

  _____

- ▪ Notes: _____

  _____

- Next Steps: _____

    _____

❏ 11. Build your child's self-esteem through counseling.

- Steps Taken: _____

    _____

- Notes: _____

    _____

- Next Steps: _____

    _____

❏ 12. Manage your child's stress.

- Steps Taken: _____

    _____

- Notes: _____

    _____

- Next Steps: _____

    _____

Tool 88: A 12-Point Multimodal Treatment Plan

Tool 89:
DSM-IV Criteria

The following list provides the criteria for diagnosis of ADHD listed in the *DSM-IV-TR*, the manual for diagnosing and treating mental health disorders. The *DSM* manual will be updated to the *DSM-V* in 2011.

Tips

Teachers and Parents: Use this list of criteria to determine the children with whom the tools in this book will be most useful.

DSM-IV Criteria

Inattentive type:

Six or more of the following symptoms of inattention have persisted for at least 6 months to a degree that is maladaptive and inconsistent with developmental level:
1. Often fails to give close attention to details or makes careless mistakes in schoolwork, work, or other activities
2. Often has difficulty sustaining attention in tasks or play activities
3. Often does not seem to listen when spoken to directly
4. Often does not follow through on instructions and fails to finish schoolwork, chores, or duties in the workplace (not due to oppositional behavior or failure to understand instructions)
5. Often has difficulty organizing tasks and activities
6. Often avoids, dislikes, or is reluctant to engage in tasks that require sustained mental effort (such as school work or homework)
7. Often loses things necessary for tasks or activities (e.g., toys, school assignments, pencils, books, or tools)
8. Is often easily distracted by extraneous stimuli
9. Is often forgetful in daily activities

Hyperactive/Impulsive type:

Six or more of the following symptoms of hyperactivity/impulsivity have persisted for at least 6 months to a degree that is maladaptive and inconsistent with developmental level:

Hyperactivity

1. Often fidgets with hands or feet or squirms in seat
2. Often leaves seat in classroom or in other situations in which remaining seated is expected
3. Often runs about or climbs excessively in situations in which it is inappropriate (in adolescents or adults, may be limited to subjective feelings of restlessness)
4. Often has difficulty playing or engaging in leisure activities quietly
5. Is often "on the go" or often acts as if "driven by a motor"
6. Often talks excessively

Impulsivity

1. Often blurts out answers before questions have been completed
2. Often has difficulty awaiting turn
3. Often interrupts or intrudes on others (e.g., butts into conversations or games)

Tool 89: DSM-IV Criteria

Tool 90:
Coexisting Conditions

ADHD, in and of itself is a challenge, but what often separates straightforward instances from those that are very challenging to manage are those who also suffer from a variety of frequently associated neuropsychiatric disorders. The frequently occurring additional diagnoses are described as *comorbidities*. According to the National Institute of Mental Health (2008b), there are several disorders that sometimes accompany childhood ADHD. The following disorders are most frequently found as coexisting disorders with ADHD in childhood (Silverman et al., 2009).

Tips

Teachers and Parents: Use this information to determine the most frequently co-occurring conditions.

Coexisting Conditions

Learning disabilities are the most common comorbidity seen with ADHD. Between 24% and 70% of all individuals with ADHD are believed to suffer from some type of learning problem (Barkley, 2006; however, it must be kept in mind that studies differ, as do the ways learning disabilities are defined). According to NIMH, approximately 20%–30% of children with ADHD also have a diagnosable specific learning disability (LD). Thus, any child seen for ADHD should be carefully screened for associated learning problems.

Language disorders, often associated with other learning problems, are diagnosed often. Expressive language deficits are seen in 10%–54% of individuals, and "pragmatic language" problems are noted 60% of the time (language pragmatics are loosely defined as language usage for the purpose of social interaction/dialogue; Barkley, 2006). Children with ADHD and associated language problems often display excessive speech, reduced fluency, and overall speech that is less logical, coherent, and organized.

Lower Average Intelligence (7–10 point deficit) in IQ testing is generally seen in ADHD children as a group. This discrepancy is felt to be due to an apparent failure to keep pace with peers academically because of the overall impact of ADHD, but also could result from poor executive functioning that partly affects IQ testing results.

Motor symptoms are another common accompanying issue in children with ADHD. These symptoms have been described as dyspraxia (motor planning). A significant population of ADHD children will have difficulty executing both fine and/or gross motor tasks such as writing, buttoning buttons or snapping snaps, tying shoelaces, or throwing and catching a ball. Formal diagnoses of these visual-motor and fine motor problems are termed a developmental coordination disorder. More than 50% of children with ADHD qualify for this diagnosis (Barkley, 2006). As a group, and linked to many of the motor issues noted above, ADHD children show reduced physical fitness, strength, and stamina.

When children are diagnosed with a **seizure disorder**, their chance of also having ADHD is 2.5 times more likely (approximately 20% of children with seizures also have ADHD; Barkley, 2006).

Sleep disorders occur in 30%–56% of children with ADHD, and the majority are mainly bedtime behavior problems, in that children with ADHD often have difficulty settling down and going to sleep without a set bedtime routine and good sleep hygiene practiced within the home. The more pronounced of these sleep initiation problems are diagnosable as delayed sleep onset disorder. Even while asleep, ADHD children move four times more frequently than their peers without ADHD (they are hyperactive even while unconscious!). Two important sleep disorders to consider when a child with ADHD has significant problems with sleep are sleep apnea and restless leg syndrome.

Motor tic disorders are seen in 10%–15% of ADHD children, with peak onset between the ages of 8 to 10 years of age (Barkley, 2006). Tourette syndrome (motor and vocal tics) is relatively rare, occurring in only 2% of children with ADHD. From another viewpoint, 50%–80% of children diagnosed with Tourette syndrome will also suffer from ADHD (this is what is termed a one-way comorbidity). People with Tourette syndrome frequently have various nervous tics and repetitive mannerisms, including eye blinks, facial twitches, or grimacing. Other individuals with Tourette syndrome may clear their throats frequently, snort, sniff, or bark out words. However, these behaviors can be controlled with medication.

Depression likely has some sort of genetic linkage to ADHD, as it appears thus far that the genetic coding for ADHD appears to create a vulnerability to major depressive disorder (MDD). Individuals with ADHD are about three times as likely to suffer a depressive disorder compared to their peers (Barkley, 2006). Many individuals with ADHD prone to developing MDD initially manifest low self-esteem in childhood, whereas the full syndrome of depression may not be fully apparent until adolescence or later.

The co-occurence of both ADHD and **bipolar disorder** (BPD) is well known, but there has been controversy as to the actual frequency. Part of this struggle may arise from the fact that differentiating between ADHD and bipolar disorder in childhood can be quite challenging. Bipolar disorder is classically characterized by moods cycling between periods of intense highs and lows.

Tool 90: Coexisting Conditions

However, in children, bipolar disorder often appears as rather chronic mood dysregulation, with a mixture of elation, depression, and irritability. Furthermore, some symptoms can be present both in ADHD and bipolar disorder. These overlapping symptoms include a high level of energy and a reduced need for sleep. Current consensus has cited the incidence of BPD in all individuals with ADHD to be between 3% and 6% (Barkley, 2006). Although teasing out the two diagnoses can be challenging, individuals rarely display some of the cardinal signs of BPD such as grandiosity, hypersexuality, and disturbed thinking, as well as actual mania. On the other hand, there may be a one-way cormorbidity (like we see in Tourette syndrome) where it has been shown that once diagnosed with BPD, there is an 80%–97% chance that the child also suffers from ADHD (E. Leibenluft, personal communication, October 2007).

Anxiety disorders co-occur with ADHD in 10%–40% of cases (Barkley, 2006). Anxiety in individuals with ADHD may be related in part to the poor emotion regulation that we commonly see in ADHD. Although legitimate anxiety disorders are likely, the most common are simple phobias or separation anxiety in early childhood. Generalized anxiety disorder becomes more common with age, and these individuals often show lower levels of impulsiveness when compared to their nonanxious ADHD peers. Additionally, when a child with these coexisting disorders receives effective treatment for ADHD it can have a positive impact on his or her anxiety, as the child will be better able to successfully complete academic tasks.

Substance abuse is a serious public health concern and a frequent comorbid condition with ADHD. Alcohol and drug abuse occur in 10%–24% of individuals with ADHD (approximately 2 to 2.5 times more often than the non-ADHD population; Barkley, 2006). There is greater use of alcohol, tobacco, and marijuana but hard drug use is related mostly to comorbid conduct disorder. It appears that substance abuse is closely tied to peer relationships with other substance-abusing peers.

Oppositional defiant disorder (ODD) is present in 40%–80% of children with ADHD (Barkley, 2006). ODD mostly affects boys, and those with the disorder often are defiant, stubborn, and noncompliant. Children with ODD frequently have temper outbursts and become belligerent. Arguing with adults and refusing to obey also is common among these children.

Approximately 20% to 40% of children with ADHD may eventually develop **conduct disorder** (CD; NIMH, 2008b). CD is thought to be an outgrowth in some children with ODD. It is a condition manifested by a persistent pattern of rule breaking and antisocial behavior and is comorbid 20%–56% of the time (Barkley, 2006). Psychopathy is seen in 20% of individuals with ADHD (Barkley, 2006). These individuals display more severe and more persistent antisocial behavior.

Note. Adapted from Silverman et al. (2009).

Tool 91: Working With Your Pediatrician

Parents often are the first to suspect that a child has ADHD. Use this information in working with your pediatrician to discuss your concerns and to know what to expect if your child is evaluated for ADHD.

Tips

Parents: Use this as a guide in working with your pediatrician in the diagnosis and treatment of ADHD.

Working With Your Pediatrician

If you are seeing core behaviors associated with ADHD in your young child, you should not delay determining if these behaviors are typical or excessive. Core symptoms include inattention, overactivity, and impulsivity. It is easy to overdiagnose or to diagnose too early, but when these symptoms occur in multiple settings and are disruptive to learning, play, and socialization they can lead to early experiences of frustration, failure, peer and adult rejection, and low self-esteem. It is unfortunate that many children are rejected from participation in preschool and kindergarten before their behavior is taken seriously. Early recognition, assessment, and management of ADHD can result in effective early intervention in the education and psychosocial development of most children with ADHD. Most families start with their general practice doctor or pediatrician when determining if their child has ADHD.

The American Academy of Pediatrics (AAP) has developed guidelines for primary care clinicians concerning the diagnosis and treatment of ADHD (Herrerias, Perrin, & Stein, 2001). These guidelines were concerned with the diagnosis of ADHD in relatively uncomplicated cases in primary care settings. Thus, these guidelines are not intended for evaluation of children with mental retardation, pervasive developmental disorder, moderate to severe sensory deficits such as visual and hearing impairment and chronic disorders associated with medications that may affect behavior, or children who have experienced physical abuse or sexual abuse.

The recommendations below are adapted from the AAP guidelines, as presented by Herrerias and colleagues (2001).

Recommendation 1

A primary care physician should request an evaluation if a child is between the ages of 6 and 12 years and displays inattention, hyperactivity, impulsivity, academic underachievement, or behavior problems. Doctors might ask questions about school performance or behavior problems at home or school.

Recommendation 2

The American Association of Pediatrics supports the use of the text revision of the fourth edition of the *Diagnostic and Statistical Manual of Mental Disorders* (*DSM-IV-TR;* APA, 2000) because the criteria have the highest level of research and clinical support.

Recommendation 3

The assessment of ADHD requires information about reported symptoms as directly obtained from parents or caregivers regarding the primary symptoms of ADHD in various settings, the child's age when the symptoms were first observed, how long they have been seen, and to what extent the symptoms impair daily life functions.

Behavior symptom information may be gathered from parents or guardians using questions about behavior, interviews, questionnaires, and rating scales. Information about the child's behavior enables some insight into family environment and parenting style so that behavior symptoms may be evaluated in the actual environment in which the child is being raised.

Questionnaires and rating scales measure the behavioral symptoms of ADHD. Rating scales are based on parents' and teachers' perceptions of core symptoms in order to discriminate between children who have ADHD and those who do not. Rating scales can be affected by the biases of the rater. In the doctor's office, it is better to use rating scales that are designed to measure ADHD and not about all of the child's behaviors.

Recommendation 4

The assessment of ADHD also requires information from the classroom teacher (or other educational staff member) regarding the main symptoms of ADHD, length of presentation of symptoms, degree of impact on daily functioning and coexisting conditions. A physician should review any reports from a school-based multidisciplinary team if possible, which will include assessments from educators. A significant part of the day of the child aged 6 to 12 is spent in school. Therefore, a description of how he or she behaves in school is important to the evaluation. With parental/guardian permission, the clinician should review school reports. It is best to receive a report from the teacher directly working with the child, who generally observes the behavior in question the most. Rating scales and questionnaires also are designed for teachers.

Other structured environments such as afterschool centers can provide ratings and observations with parent/guardian permission. If children are home-schooled, further evidence of core behavior symptoms in settings should be obtained. Often, significant differences exist between parent and teacher ratings, but the finding of such a discrepancy does not preclude the diagnosis of ADHD. Further sources that can be helpful in determining if the child meets *DSM-IV* criteria is to obtain reports from former teachers, religious leaders, or athletic coaches.

Recommendation 5

The assessment of the child with ADHD should include the investigation of coexisting conditions. Up to one third of children with ADHD have one or more coexisting conditions. (See Tool 90 for more on coexisting conditions.)

Many coexisting conditions may be apparent to the primary care clinician. For example, sadness and the preference for isolation may alert the doctor to the possibility of depressive symptoms. A history of anxiety in family members or frequent fears and problems with separation may reflect an anxiety disorder. Poor school achievement may suggest a learning disability. Psychological and educational testing may be necessary in order to determine whether there is a discrepancy between the child's potential and academic progress, often partly reflecting the possibility of a learning disability, especially if there has already been resistance to individualized interventions.

Recommendation 6

Some cases are straightforward and do not regularly require testing, although testing may reveal coexisting conditions. Not every child requires a full evaluation by a psychiatrist and/or psychologist. It is the opinion of the AAP that other diagnostic tests do not contribute to establishing the diagnosis of ADHD. There is very little proof to support regular screenings of children for high lead levels, thyroid function, or electroencephalography as part the diagnosis for ADHD. Continuous performance tests, which look like reaction time type electronic measures are not supported by research, because the AAP has found that they have limited ability to tell the difference between children with ADHD and comparison control groups.

After a diagnosis has been made, medication may be prescribed. It is very important to monitor behavior changes that the medication is prescribed for or the absence of change and any side effects. The physician should be informed of the results of these medications. Often parents become frustrated because the medication is not strong enough or too powerful, and they may give up or the child may give up before giving feedback to the physician. Sometimes a specialist is needed to reconsider medications, such as a child psychiatrist or a developmental behavioral pediatric specialist. It is very important that the parent and physician have a workable, ongoing relationship so that the child's response to medications and other interventions are continuously monitored. Use simple graphs or charts made at home or produced at school to display and monitor medication effects if these are found helpful.

Keep your doctor in the loop so as to work with the child's case manager if one has been established at school, home, or another practice. There can be a good back and forth communication between doctors using notes and IEP and 504 Plan documents or include your doctor in IEP meetings with conference calls when needed.

Tool 91: Working With Your Pediatrician

Tool 92:
College Planning

Continuing to offer support and guidance and, at the same time, expecting the adolescent to apply his or her emerging self-advocacy and responsible behavior to a postsecondary setting is important.

It is imperative for the student with ADHD who has relied on modifications and accommodations in the past to act proactively; this includes choosing the right college, technical school, or profession. In August of 2008, The Higher Education Opportunity Act (HEOA) was passed, which included the establishment of a coordinating center to develop inclusive comprehensive transition and postsecondary programs for students with disabilities. This new authorization will allow students with disabilities such as ADHD an easier transition to the post high school years.

Tips

Teachers and Parents: Teachers, share this with parents so that they will be active participants in the college selection process. Parents, set clear parameters around which your child can make choices, including cost and distance. Students should use this tool to take notes during the college planning process.

College Planning

Talk to high school counselors or private counselors who work with students with learning difficulties and students who have been through the college search.

Options I am considering:

2-year colleges:

4-year colleges:

Technical:

Level of competitiveness:

Location:

Size:

Special services I need in a college:
- ❏ Departments and learning centers dedicated to serving students with special needs
- ❏ Mentors/Case managers
- ❏ Programs providing direct instruction
- ❏ Other services I need:

_____

_____

_____

Services available at the college I'm considering:
- ❏ Departments and learning centers dedicated to serving students with special needs
- ❏ Mentors/Case managers
- ❏ Programs providing direct instruction
- ❏ Other:

_____

_____

_____

Notes:

Tool 92: College Planning

Tool 93:
College Selection

Students with ADHD need assistance from parents in determining the appropriate college environment.

Tips

Teachers: Offer parents this tool as their student plans for college.

Parents: Be an active participant in the college selection process. Set clear parameters around which your child can make choices, including cost and distance.

College Selection

Criteria	College A	College B	College C	College D
Location				
Cost				
Majors				
School and Class Size				

Tool 93: College Selection

Criteria	College A	College B	College C	College D
Criteria for Admission				
Documents Required (IEP, etc.)				
Support Services				
Child's Positive Reaction				
Child's Negative Reaction				
Parent's Positive Reaction				
Parent's Negative Reaction				

Note. Adapted from Harman (2001).

Tool 94:
College Strategies Checklist

This checklist helps increase the likelihood of a positive college experience.

Tips

Teachers: Offer parents this tool as they plan for their child to go to college or provide this tool directly to the student.

Parents: Use this checklist with your child to ensure a more successful college experience.

College Strategies Checklist

- ❏ I am a self-advocate.
  - ▪ I know my strengths and needs.
  - ▪ I know my legal rights.
  - ▪ I arrange for campus services.
  - ▪ I communicate with my professors and other staff.

- ❏ I am aware of how my ADHD affects my performance.
  - ▪ Organization
  - ▪ Functioning in my environment
  - ▪ Academic achievement
  - ▪ Campus activities
  - ▪ Other

- ❏ I arrange for, accept, and implement appropriate adaptations, accommodations, and services.
- ❏ I develop time management skills.
- ❏ I develop organizational skills.
- ❏ I set priorities.
- ❏ I get help when necessary.

Tool 95:
College Skills Checklist

This checklist provides suggestions for getting support in college, choosing classes, studying, and organizing.

Tips

Parents: Give this to your student. Have him go to the office responsible for LD programs or services, introduce himself, and find out what he must do to be eligible for services and what is available. It will be much easier to receive help later if he needs it once he has visited this office.

College Skills Checklist

Be Prepared

- ❏ Inform your advisor that you have special needs. Ask for help in choosing small, structured classes with professors who use multisensory methods of instruction, provide a syllabus, and present information clearly and in an organized fashion.
- ❏ Inform your professors of your needs early in the semester (or ask for help from your advisor or LD office). Most professors will be receptive to your needs if alerted to them before there is a problem.
- ❏ Be encouraged to choose instructors who provide visual as well as auditory input during their lectures.

Class Suggestions

- ❏ Do not hesitate to question the professors if you don't understand. They all should have office hours. It is important not to let this go, as the next lecture is apt to build upon the class before.
- ❏ Ask for help in finding a note-taking buddy to go over lecture material or access the notes on the Internet as posted by your professors. Many schools are now making provisions for this service.
- ❏ Participate in class discussions. This can bring up your grade if you have trouble with tests.
- ❏ Attend all quiz and review sessions. If possible, join or create a study group to discuss and review material for each course.

❑ Make use of tutorial services immediately if you have trouble with the content of a course or if you need help with assignments.

❑ Sit at the center front of the classroom. This will automatically eliminate much of the auditory and visual distraction and make it easier to focus upon the instructor.

❑ Peripheral stimulation can be distracting. Keep unnecessary materials off of your desk. Extraneous materials should be put away immediately after use.

Study Skills

❑ Index cards are excellent aids for memorization of facts. (Put one fact per card and use them like flash cards until you know them. Return to them later for review before tests.) They also are useful in organizing notes for a paper. Highlighters also are effective for this purpose.

❑ Establish a set time and place to study relatively free from distractions.

❑ Use a large calendar to plot due dates and daily increments of assignments. Be sure to place all other important activities on the calendar also so that you may plan around them.

❑ Ensure in class that homework assignments have been noted and understood before leaving for the day. Check with classmates if any assignments are unclear.

❑ Break down large tasks into smaller clear chunks, which can be reviewed and monitored sequentially.

❑ Utilize a work sample as examples to work from. These often are available online.

❑ Focus study on main ideas.

Organizational Skills

❑ For nonroutine tasks develop a simple calendar and to do list.
❑ For routine tasks utilize a daily responsibilities list.
❑ Anticipate problem situations and activities.
❑ Highly structured routines and specific instructions are beneficial.

Support

You may benefit from tutoring to increase the efficiency and accuracy of your reading college material and in overcoming your difficulty in memorizing or applying the rules of mathematics. Look into the following support services found at many universities:

❑ Test accommodations

- ❏ Priority registration
- ❏ Adaptive computer labs
- ❏ Support groups
- ❏ Tutoring on test-taking strategies
- ❏ Organization assistance
- ❏ Time management guidance

Tool 96:
Obtaining Assistance in College

This tool provides information about getting academic assistance at the college level.

Tips

Parents: Some colleges only require a prior IEP or 504 Plan from high school to receive services. As a general rule, an IEP, 504 Plan, or evaluation should not be more than 3 years old.

Obtaining Assistance in College

In order to apply for services from the disabilities office as a student with ADHD, a recent ADHD psychoeducational assessment for college accommodations often is required. Such an evaluation typically requires an assessment of intellectual functioning, learning style, and academic strengths and weaknesses. The process of applying for services and the procedure for reviewing a student's eligibility for services differs among the various colleges and universities. Students who have been diagnosed with ADHD are able to choose whether or not to disclose their condition during the admissions process. Sometimes the general application includes an opportunity, but not a requirement, to disclose and apply for disability services. If, however, applying for the disabilities services program is a separate process, which it frequently is, the student will benefit from completing the application at the same time as she applies for admission to the college or shortly after she is accepted for admission to the college. Often, students decide to provide documentation in the general application because this information can help the college understand their strengths, while taking into account any weaknesses that can be explained by the ADHD diagnosis. The submission of documents does not guarantee that a student with ADHD is eligible for special services in college.

In submitting documentation for a disability, the following documents are commonly required (Silverman et al., 2009):

✓ A letter from a professional describing the disability and discussing the current academic impact

✓ A recent psychological evaluation that diagnoses the disability and states the date of the diagnosis

✓ A current IEP or 504 Plan from high school that documents the provided accommodations and services

Tool 97:
Quieting the Mind With Yoga: Yoga as an Adjunct for ADHD Management

Research supports the benefits of yoga in improving symptoms of ADHD.

Tips

Parents and Teachers: Individuals with ADHD may find yoga to be a useful tool in cultivating physiological calm.

Quieting the Mind With Yoga: Yoga as an Adjunct for ADHD Management

The physical practice of yoga, now popularized in spas and fitness clubs for its numerous health benefits, is rooted in ancient Indian traditions with dramatically different and noble intentions: the goal of stilling the mind. Many Western practitioners of yoga seek out the health-generating benefits of the "asana" (physical) and the "pranayama" (breathing) practices. What fewer practitioners know is that these practices were designed so as to create more optimal disease-free conditions in which to develop psychological health and peace of mind through improved concentration and meditation. The word "yoga" means "union," "to yoke," and "to tie the strands of the mind together" (Desikachar, 1995, p. 5). In fact, the definitive text on the philosophy of yoga offers the following definition: "Yoga is the stilling of the fluctuations of the mind" (Desikachar, 1995, p. 5).

Devoted yogis can spend decades understanding, exploring, and mastering the various technical components of yoga. Common benefits of the regular and committed practice can include improved strength and flexibility, improved function of internal organs and systems, a sense of vitality and relaxation, and mental calm.

Even novices, regardless of age, fitness level, or health status, can experience immediate benefit from some simple yoga exercises. Following are some simple exercises to try. It is helpful to wear loose-fitting clothing and to practice on a yoga mat. These exercises are useful in creating a sense of inner calm.

Cat/Cow

Position yourself on your hands and knees, with your hands directly under your shoulders and your knees directly under your hips. As you take a deep breath in, look up toward the ceiling and tilt your tailbone up while you allow your belly to drop. As you exhale, round your spine as you look down toward your navel. Repeat three to four more times, continuing to match your movements with your inhales and exhales. This warm-up helps to loosen the spine and prepares you for more vigorous movement.

Downward Facing Dog

While on your hands and knees, tuck your toes under, extend your arms long with your fingers spread wide and slowly lift your hips up toward the sky. Slowly straighten your legs and drop your heels down toward the Earth. While in this upside-down "V" position, concentrate on gliding your shoulder blades down your back and on breathing deeply in and out. This is a strength-building position that helps stretch out your entire back.

Hanging Forward Bend

Beginning in a Downward Facing Dog position, slowly walk your feet in toward your hands. Once your feet reach the top of the mat, you can keep your knees bent as you let your hands gravitate toward the Earth. Inhale as you slowly straighten your legs and exhale to create more space in your spine as it lengthens. If you wish, grab opposite elbows and slowly pendulum your arms from side to side. Like other forward bends, this position stretches the hamstrings and back, blocks out external stimulation, and creates a sensation of mental calm.

Mountain Pose

Beginning in a Hanging Forward Bend, draw your navel toward your spine, bend your knees and slowly roll up to stand. Stand with your feet hip-width apart and roll your shoulders back and down. Draw up through the crown of your head to lengthen your neck and spine. Turn your palms to face forward with your arms by your sides. Gaze forward. This pose cultivates inner stability, confidence, and poise.

Tree Pose

While standing in Mountain Pose, lift one foot off the ground, and draw the sole of that foot to the inside of your standing leg. You can either press it firmly against your inner thigh, your calf, or your ankle. Draw your hands together in a prayer position, and concentrate on a fixed point in front of you in order to maintain balance. This pose strengthens core muscles and improves balance and concentration. After doing this pose on one foot, repeat on the other side.

Deep Abdominal Breathing

Sit in a comfortable cross-legged position. Place your palms on your belly and focus on observing the movement of your hands as your belly rises and falls with each breath. After noticing the natural movement, focus on slowly extending the length of each inhale and exhale. Focus on having the breath originate in the belly as opposed to the upper chest or shoulders. This is a very calming exercise that promotes a meditative state.

A Note About Working With Kids

Kids of all ages respond to yoga as long as the exercises are catered toward their needs. Children particularly enjoy practicing animal shapes (e.g., cat, cow, dog) and even using their imagination to create new shapes with new names. Children should be encouraged to use their imaginations when practicing yoga. Unlike with adults, where the emphasis often is on proper alignment aligned with the breath, yoga with kids is focused more on experimenting with play-filled movement in a safe, noncompetitive atmosphere.

Trained children's yoga instructors are available to help create appropriate routines for different age groups.

Tool 98:
Encouraging Achievement
at Home

This tool provides parents with suggestions of how to instill a positive and effective attitude around the learning process and daily activities in the home environment.

Tips

Parents: Students' poor school performance may or may not be related to their disability. Whatever the cause, they may be displaying underachievement. Frequently, parents may be so careful to ensure protection for their children with disabilities that they fail to set high standards for them. We are not suggesting that children with disabilities should be pushed beyond their limits. Many persons unfamiliar with the complexities of special education issues may oversimplify problems with achievement by suggesting that "if she worked harder, she would be fine." Underachievement can be a problem at all ability levels, whether students are disabled or not. It is important to remember that adults are responsible to some extent for their own happiness, but children require emotional protection and have a right to experience happiness. They also require moral, character, and spiritual guidance to make positive life choices. The push toward commonly assumed markers of achievement (such as grades and SAT scores) should not violate their rights for emotional protection, the experience of happiness, or the ability to think for themselves about their life purposes (Silverman et al., 2009).

Encouraging Achievement at Home

Parental attitude in the home is the key to encouraging school achievement. We hope we love our children unconditionally, but every child can be frustrating at times. For that reason, parents need to continually evaluate their feelings toward their child. At times, parents may harbor feelings of resentment or even rejection toward their child with ADHD, which in turn are responsible for guilty feelings and irrational responses. Are there barriers to demonstrating unconditional love?

Parents can be conveying unconditional love to their child even when they are disagreeing or correcting their child's behavior. Remember, a child's behavior might be bad, but the child isn't. For too many children, shame results from feeling as though they are fundamentally bad. Shame, even for short periods, is one of the most destructive emotions a child can feel. Making a child with disabilities feel shame for something out of his control is abusive. There are parents whose ability to love their child is temporarily blocked due to their own concerns, anxieties, and frustrations. This is, in some way, to be expected when one is rearing a child with ADHD. Honesty with one's self is very important. There is no perfect way to feel about the situation. Just remember that love emerges when the truth is confronted honestly.

Here are some further pointers for encouraging achievement:

- ✓ Every child can be seen as a unique gift with unique potential.
- ✓ Avoid comparing the child to other children. Let the child know that he has a duty to know his own strengths and make his best efforts in and out of the classroom. Not every child can be the best at everything, but he can be his best at something. Many very competent children have low expectations for themselves because the bar has been set too low. This is especially the case in children with disabilities—too many parents are happy to see their children just getting by. If a child is currently an underachiever, convey the firm belief and expectation that she can learn and excel.
- ✓ A parent's attitude toward school can make all the difference in a child's achievement. Convey to the child that school is an honorable place, that teachers are worthy of respect, and that learning is their major job, second only to being a good human being.
- ✓ Directly explain the importance of good grades as a pathway to achievement in obtaining life's long-term rewards.
- ✓ Familiarize yourself with special education law.
- ✓ Attend all school meetings regarding the assessment and recommended educational supports for your child.
- ✓ In being a reasonable advocate, be sure that accommodations, supports, and special instructional strategies are in place to make learning easier, but do not relieve the child from her responsibility to make reasonable efforts.
- ✓ Know your child's strengths and weaknesses. Eventually, a child's strengths will emerge, coalesce, and integrate into a unique mix that many parents enjoy and treasure and will lead to the child's feeling of competence and accomplishment. Obtaining psychological, educational, and other assessments can help clarify your child's strengths and needs.
- ✓ Decrease marital and family conflict that can cause roadblocks and resistance to emotional growth and motivation to learn.
- ✓ Adult partners should talk about their views and expectations of their children and their family priorities.

✓ Parents should never argue about their child in front of him or her.

✓ Parents should seek to maximize points of agreement and learn to agree where they disagree. Put the "small stuff" aside. Make discussions a safe place to forge a shared philosophy about child rearing. Try to be on the same page as much as possible about child rearing practices, rules, and consequences. When there are great disparities between parental expectations, children lock up or learn to fail as a way to passively punish parents for not communicating effectively.

✓ Provide a sense of harmony in the home that fosters a desire to be there. Try to eat one meal together daily as a family and plan at-home family events such as regular game or movie nights.

✓ Get help with your child's behavior problems with parent training. Parent training can help parents learn how to appropriately respond to their child's frustrating behaviors and they can learn calm discipline techniques to effectively address these behaviors. Parent-to-parent training is available at many CHADD local chapters. Additionally, some psychologists and other mental health professionals can provide parent training.

✓ Parents may seek counseling to help minimize disagreements and lessen tension in the home over other issues.

✓ Success feels good. Children are born loving to learn and master challenges. Reward a child's successes with praise in a meaningful and genuine way so that she learns to know the feeling derived from mastering her challenges.

✓ Activities with intrinsic incentives often are higher and more enduring rewards than prizes.

✓ Be patient with the child. A positive self-concept as a learner takes time for a child who has been experiencing little success. It may take a while before the positive experience of academic success takes hold.

✓ Limit television and video game time to one hour per weekday and 1 ½ hours per weekend day. Parents also should limit telephone, texting, instant messaging, and computer time.

✓ Make sure the child gets adequate sleep by turning in nightly at a reasonable hour. Try not to break this rule on the weekends.

✓ Be open to mental health consultation for significant problems and to parent counseling.

✓ Make sure the child knows the rules for home behavior and responsibilities. Have them written out and posted in the child's room until she has mastered them.

✓ Remember that children see structure and limits as part of being loved. They are uncomfortable, confused, and even frightened without clear limits and expectations.

Tool 98: Encouraging Achievement at Home

✓ Develop a "To Do" list to post inside the child's bedroom door with a check-off system. Parents may want to update this weekly as the child receives assignments from school or even daily.

✓ Be a benevolent dictator first, and a friend later, when rules are established. Freedom should be earned through demonstrated responsibility.

✓ Parents should model the behavior and values expected from the child in their own day-to-day activities, behavior, and conversation.

✓ Regularly demonstrate affection, especially with teenagers. Parents should tell their children often that they love them.

✓ Evaluate the openness of communication with the child through regular conversations. Children need to feel a parent's benign presence and acceptance through regular communication.

✓ Parents should be in regular contact with their child's school. Try to keep one teacher, special educator, administrator, or counselor as a pivotal information conduit. Use voicemail, e-mail, or any form of communication that is convenient for the school representative, and always communicate on an agreed-upon schedule for setting up meetings about the child. Establish good communication boundaries with your school representative and stick to them.

✓ Check that the child has homework. If the child is lying about homework, that is still a lie and a serious problem, even if it is a little lie.

✓ Parents should set up homework rules and guidelines.

✓ Come to an agreement with the child on regular study times every day for homework.

✓ Break up homework periods with dinner, snack, or exercise breaks.

✓ Encourage the child to communicate about homework problems or questions with friends through telephone, instant messaging, or study groups.

✓ Volunteer to help out at school at least once a month, even with (or especially with) menial tasks. Let the school staff provide you with the work they need done. Volunteering should be controlled by the school and not by the parents' ideas of what the school needs. Volunteering shows children that their parents value school as a part of their community.

✓ Attend at least one PTA or school function quarterly.

✓ Never miss a Back to School Night or teacher/parent conference.

✓ Find validity about the child's needs by obtaining solid data as might be supplied by regular school testing or individualized psychological and/or educational assessments as required.

✓ Home responsibilities and chores are important, but should take second place to homework.

✓ At night, place everything needed for the next day's schoolwork in the child's backpack next to the front or back door, so it can't be forgotten the next morning.

✓ Read to or with a young child every night. Children should see their parents reading at home (even newspapers and magazines convey the importance of reading).

✓ Develop a timetable for improved grades.

✓ Encourage the child to be unafraid to associate with and play with high-achieving children. Parents have a right to express their approval or concern about their child's friends.

✓ Encourage the child to have extracurricular activities at school. Concentrate on activities that the child actually enjoys to make school a desirable place to be.

✓ Overall, remember that parents are their child's first and most important teachers. Parenting is a great art, as well as responsibility. You will feel proud later that you have made your children a high priority.

✓ Parents do play a key role in helping children adjust and master their worlds. This can be particularly challenging when the symptoms of ADHD inhibit practical, functional daily adjustment.

✓ Parents are to be commended for their efforts, flexibility, perseverance, and creativity in child rearing with kids who present challenges. They need to also realize that they cannot do it all alone and need to network, utilize, and create community supports for their children.

✓ Attend support groups like Children and Adults with Attention Deficit Hyperactivity Disorder (CHADD) where available or help create one in the area. CHADD is a national volunteer organization that is very helpful to families of individuals with ADHD. Each local CHADD affiliate may offer some of the following services:

  ▪ free monthly support group meetings,
  ▪ special events and conferences,
  ▪ local resource information (including a resource table in the back of the meeting room for local advertising of products/services),
  ▪ public education and outreach, and
  ▪ parent-to-parent training classes.

Note. Adapted from Silverman et al. (2009).

Tool 98: Encouraging Achievement at Home

Tool 99:
Other Conditions That
Resemble ADHD

There are many other life situations and conditions that may resemble ADHD.

Tips

Parents: It is important to keep in mind that other conditions can have symptoms similar to ADHD.

Other Conditions That Resemble ADHD

When making the diagnosis of ADHD, it is a professional's first responsibility to gather enough information to rule out possible reasons for the child's behavior. In ruling out other potential causes for the ADHD-like symptoms, the National Institute of Mental Health (NIMH, 2008a) emphasized that it is important for professionals to examine the child's school and medical records when making a diagnosis.

Among other possible causes for symptoms similar to ADHD are the following:

✓ a sudden change in the child's life including the death of a close family member such as a parent or grandparent, his parents' divorce, or a parent's loss of his or her job;

✓ undetected seizures in the child, such as petit mal or temporal lobe seizures;

✓ a middle ear infection suffered by the child that causes intermittent hearing problems;

✓ other medical disorders that the child has that may affect brain functioning;

✓ underachievement in the child caused by a learning disability;

✓ childhood anxiety or depression;

✓ hearing or vision problems;

✓ an unusually stressful or chaotic home or classroom environment; and

✓ abuse or neglect.

Note. Adapted from Silverman et al. (2009).

Tool 100:
Understanding Statistical Terms in Your Child's Testing Reports

This tool provides a guide for understanding the terminology that often is present in school and private testing reports.

Tips

Parents: Some parents and teachers find statistical comparisons to be confusing. The following terms help to explain language and graphs that usually accompany test scores. These are adapted from the American Educational Research Association, American Psychological Association, and National Council on Measurement in Education (1999).

Understanding Statistical Terms In Your Child's Testing Reports

Ability/Achievement Discrepancy: Ability/Achievement discrepancy methods are procedures for comparing an individual's current academic performance to others of the same age or grade with the same ability score. The ability score could be based on the general intellectual ability score (cognitive score), IQ score, or other ability score. Scores for each academic area are compared to cognitive ability scores in one of these areas to see if the individual is achieving at the level one would expect based on his intellectual ability level. (This is no longer the only measure used to explore why a student is achieving above or below expectations, but is a valuable source of information. It is important to use the same measurement when comparing ability to achievement and this is usually expressed in "standard scores" to be explained below.)

Achievement Levels/Proficiency Levels: Descriptions of an individual's skills level in a particular area of knowledge or skill, usually defined as degrees on a scale, often labeled from "basic" to "advanced," that represent broad ranges for classifying performance. The exact labeling of these categories may vary from one test to another. (It is always best when a range is reported from high to low in a band and not only the single score in the particular test result.)

Achievement Test: A test designed to measure the extent to which a person has acquired certain knowledge and/or skills that have been taught in school or as a part of some other planned instruction or training. An achievement test reflects progress in a specific, acquired skill and is not a measure of the limits of a person's ability.

Age-Based Norms: These norms were developed for the purpose of comparing a student's score with the scores obtained by other students at the same age on the same test. The student's standing or rank within the age reference group determines how much a student knows. For example, a norms table for 12-year-old students would provide information such as the percentage of 12-year-olds (based on a nationally representative sample) who scored at or below each score value on a particular test. It is very important to understand test score terms when comparing a child's progress to other children or to the child's own scores over time. Generally speaking, the best comparisons on standardized tests have scales or "norms" that are based on age. This makes developmental comparisons more meaningful. When we compare children to others in the same grade, we may be comparing them to kids who are younger or older in the same grade.

Age Equivalent: The age for which a given score is the median (middle) score. An examinee with an age equivalent of 7.5 indicates that he or she received the same score (raw score, scale score, standard score, etc.) as the average child who is 7 years, 5 months old.

Aptitude Test: A test designed to measure the ability of a person to develop skills or acquire knowledge. Any test used to assess a person's "readiness" to learn or potential for future success in a particular area if the appropriate education or training is provided (e.g., musical aptitude test). An IQ test is a well-known example of an aptitude test for measuring general academic ability (but the term "aptitude" is most frequently used to describe specific skills or talents).

Average: Any statistic indicating the central tendency or most typical score of a set of scores, such as the arithmetic mean, median, and mode. The term average, without qualifications as to type, typically refers to the arithmetic mean. In predicting anything, the best guess where all other information is lacking is the average, most frequently referred to statistically as the "mean."

Basal: For individually administered tests, the point on a test, associated with a given level of functioning or skill, for which an examiner is confident that all items before that item would be answered correctly (considered too easy). The items below this point, although not administered to the individual student, are given full credit. This is a starting point where it is assumed the person being tested can perform without a problem.

Battery: A set of tests, generally standardized on the same population, and designed to be administered together as a unit. The scores on these tests can be readily compared or used in combination for decision making. In other words, scores can be computed and interpreted for each individual test as well as the entire battery.

Ceiling: The upper limit of ability that a test can measure. Individual or groups scoring at or near the highest possible score are said to have "reached the ceiling" of the test. For individually administered tests, the ceiling refers to the point during administration after which all other items will no longer be answered correctly (considered too difficult), and results in the examiner stopping the administration of the test.

Cognitive Assessment: The process of systematically gathering test scores and related data in order to make judgments about an individual's ability to perform various mental activities involved in the processing, learning, retention, conceptualization, and organization of sensory, perceptual, verbal, spatial, and motor (and other intellectual) abilities.

Composite Score: A score that is derived by combining one or more subscores. This typically is accomplished by averaging or summing the contributing scores, which often are weighted according to their relative importance. For example, a reading composite might include many kinds of reading measures like word recognition and comprehension.

Confidence Interval: An interval or range between two values on a scale within which a specified score is found. An individual's test score provides a good estimate of the student's ability in a specific area. However, this estimate, as in any measurement process, contains some degree of error (either for or against the student's favor). A confidence interval provides a range of values around the estimate to indicate how accurate or precise the estimate is likely to be. The confidence level associated with the score interval, usually 68%, 85%, 90%, or 95%, indicates the percentage of times, given repeated sampling, that the interval will contain the student's true score.

Correlation: The degree of relationship (or strength of association) between two sets of scores, based on the same set of individuals. The relationship can be positively correlated (e.g., students scoring high on one test also tend to score high on the other), negatively correlated (e.g., students scoring low on one test tend to score high on the other), or zero correlated (e.g., lack of any relationship between the scores). Correlation simply refers to the strength of the relationship existing between two sets of values and does not necessarily imply that one influenced the other or caused the other to happen. The most commonly used statistic for measuring correlation is Pearson's product-moment correlation, r (Pearson's correlation coefficient).

Criterion-Referenced Test (CRT): A test designed to measure a student's performance as compared to an expected level of mastery, educational objective, or standard. The type of scores resulting from this type of test provide information on what a student knows or can do with respect to a given content area as opposed to a score indicating how that student ranks among his or her age or grade peers (norm group).

Grade Equivalents: These are expressed in terms of grade and months into grade, assuming a 9-month school year (e.g., 8.4 means after 4 months of instruction in the eighth grade). The grade equivalent corresponding to a given score on any test indicates the test performance of the average student at that grade level at a certain time of the year. Because of this, grade equivalents are not based on an equal interval scale, and therefore cannot be added, subtracted, or averaged across test levels the way other scores can (scale scores or standard scores). For comparison see age equivalent.

IQ Test: An intelligence test administered to measure an individual's IQ (intelligence quotient). IQ scores originally were expressed as the ratio of an examinee's mental age to his or her chronological age, although over the years, that formula has been replaced with the concept of the deviation IQ (e.g., a standard score with a mean of 100 and a standard deviation of 15 or 16).

Longitudinal: Dealing with the growth or change of an individual or group over time. Refers to a type of reporting style that displays the current test scores and test scores from previous years along with information pertaining to the amount of change or rate of growth (e.g., differences in developmental standard scores, grade equivalents, etc.) that is indicated from one year to another.

Median: The middle point (score) in a distribution of scores that divides the group into two equal parts, each part containing 50% of the data. The median corresponds to the 50th percentile. Half of the scores are below the median and half are above it, except when the median itself is one of the obtained scores. For example, the median of the set {4, 7, 8, 9, 10, 10, 12} is 9.

Mode: The score that occurs most frequently in a distribution of scores.

Normal Distribution: Also known as the bell-shaped curve because of its distinctive appearance in that scores are distributed symmetrically about the middle, such that there are an equal number of scores above as below the mean, with more scores concentrated near the middle than at the extremes. The normal distribution is a theoretical distribution defined by specific mathematical properties that many human traits and psychological characteristics appear to closely approximate (e.g., height, weight, intelligence). Some features of the normal distribution are: (1) The mean, median, and mode are identical in value; (2) The scores are distributed symmetrical about the mean (50.0% above the mean and 50.0% below the mean); (3) 68.26% of the scores are within 1 standard deviation of the mean (34.13% above the mean and 34.13% below the mean); (4) 95.44% of the scores are within 2 standard deviations of the mean (47.72% above the mean and 47.72% below the mean); (5) 99.72% of the scores are within 3 standard deviations of the mean (49.86% above the mean and 49.86% below the mean).

Norm-Referenced Interpretation: A score interpretation based on a comparison of a test taker's performance to the performance of other people in a specified reference population (e.g., age groups, grade groups). Norm-referenced interpretations can be for individuals (i.e., student norms) or for institutions (e.g., school norms) and could involve converting scores to scale scores (or standard scores), percentile ranks, stanines, or grade equivalents depending on the use of the test and the information provided by the test publisher. Norm-referenced interpretations allow educators to get a look at the performance of their students in relation to the rest of the nation.

Percentile Rank (PR): The percentage of scores in a specified distribution that fall at or below the point of a given score. Percentile ranks range in value from 1 to 99, and indicate the status or relative standing of an individual within a specified group (e.g., norms group), by indicating the percent of individuals in that group who obtained lower scores. For example, if a student earned a 72nd percentile rank in Language, this would mean he or she scored as well as or better than 72% of the students in a particular norm group who were administered that same test of Language. This also implies that only 28% (100 – 72) of the norm group scored the same or higher than this student. Note however, an individual's percentile rank can vary depending on which group is used to determine the ranking. A student is simultaneously a member of many groups: classroom, grade, building, school district, state, and nation. Test developers typically publish different sets of percentile ranks to permit schools to make the most relevant comparisons possible. Generally speaking, standard scores are more accurate because they are not as biased by a particular population's distribution.

Quartile: One of three points (defined as low, middle, or upper), which divide the scores in a distribution into four equal groups, each containing 25% of the data. Quartiles are special cases of percentiles—the lower, middle, and upper quartiles correspond to the 25th, 50th (median), and 75th percentiles.

Reliability: The degree to which test scores for a group of examinees are consistent over repeated administrations of the same test, and therefore considered dependable and repeatable for an individual examinee. A test that produces highly consistent, stable results (i.e., relatively free from random error) is said to be highly reliable. The reliability of a test typically is expressed as a reliability coefficient or by the standard error of measurement derived by that coefficient.

Speed or Rate Test: A test in which performance is primarily measured by the time taken to perform a specified task or by the number of tasks performed in an allotted amount of time. A speed test also refers to a test scored for accuracy, while the test taker works under time pressure. Typing tests and tests of reading speed (e.g., number of words per minute) are two examples of speed tests. In an educational testing context, the item difficulties of a speed test are generally such that given no specified time limit, all test takers should be able to complete all test items correctly. Rate is very rarely measured in many reading tests. Persons with problems with rate of performance may require accommodations for extended time in testing if they qualify with some categories of disability (e.g., learning disability, ADHD, or some emotional conditions).

Standard Age Scores (SAS): Normalized standard scores, having a mean of 100 and a standard deviation of 15 or 16, provided for each battery and composite. These scores are developed for the purpose of comparing the rate and level of cognitive development of an individual to other students in the same age group. The standard age score can be converted to other derived scores such as age percentile rank (APR) and age stanines (AS) through the use of a set of conversion tables.

Standard Deviation (SD): A statistic that measures the degree of spread or dispersion of a set of scores. The value of this statistic is always greater than or equal to zero. If all of the scores in a distribution are identical, the standard deviation is equal to zero. The further the scores are away from each other in value, the greater the standard deviation. This statistic is calculated from using the information about the deviations (distances) between each score and the distribution's mean.

Standard Score (SS): A type of derived score, which is a transformation of the raw score, and whose score distribution in a specified population has convenient, known values for the mean and standard deviation. Often this term is used to specifically denote z-scores (mean = 0.0 and standard deviation = 1.0), and any linear transformation of z-scores. However, standard scores also can be developed to provide a continuous score scale (developmental scale) across different levels and forms of a test. Standard scores permit the direct comparison of examinees by placement of the scores on a common scale and, for this reason, are useful for longitudinal comparisons. The terms scale score and standard score often are used interchangeably—even though these scores may be derived by different methods, their purpose and use can be similar.

Stanine: The name stanine is simply a derivation of the standard-nine scale. Stanines are normalized standard scores, ranging in value from 1–9, whose distribution has a mean of 5 and a standard deviation of 2. Stanines 2 through 8 are equal to a ½ standard deviation unit in width, with the middle stanine of 5 defined as the range of scores ¼ of a standard deviation below to ¼ of a standard deviation above the mean. Stanines can, more easily, be thought of as coarse groupings of percentile ranks, and like percentile ranks, indicate the relative rank of a score within a particular group. Due to their coarseness, stanines are less precise indicators than percentile ranks, at times can be misleading, and are rarely used in education.

T-Scores: T-scores are a direct transformation of z-scores and range (roughly) from 20 to 80 (corresponding to approximately 3 standard deviations above and below the mean).

Validity: The degree to which tests measure what they are designed to measure. There are various ways of assessing validity, depending on the type of test and its intended use.

Z-score: A type of standard score such that the distribution of the scores for a specified population has a mean of 0.0 and a standard deviation of 1.0. The z-score indicates the amount a student's score (X) deviates from the mean in relation to the standard deviation (SD) of the group. For example, if a student's score is 25, and the group's mean and standard deviation are 15 and 5, respectively, then the student's z score would be 2.0, indicating that the student scored 2 standard deviations above the group mean.

This information will help you as you deal with graphs like the following:

Interpretation of Evaluation Results

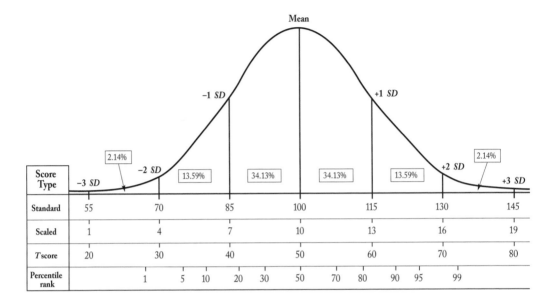

Tool 101:
Sample Letter to Request Accommodations or Services

This tool provides a model letter that can be used to request a meeting to discuss the possibility of your child receiving accommodations or services at school.

Tips

Parents: This template may be used for a letter to the appropriate personnel when requesting accommodations and/or services for your child.

Sample Letter to Request Accommodations or Services

Date: _____

Dear _____:
    (principal's name)

I am the parent of _____, who was born on _____
    (student's name)   *(date of birth)*

and is in the _____ grade at _____.
    (grade)   *(school)*

_____ was recently diagnosed with Attention Deficit
    (student's name)

Hyperactivity Disorder by_____. Since _____
    (name of professional)   *(name of student)*

began school, teachers have reported concerns related to _____'s
    (name of student)

academic performance and behavior. Specific issues have been raised regarding

_____'s _____
    (name of student)   *(brief description of areas of reported difficulty)*

My child is not achieving to _____ full potential and may need services

(his or her)

and accommodations. Therefore, I am requesting a comprehensive multidisciplinary evaluation to determine if my child meets the eligibility requirements for special education services and/or related services under either IDEA in the "Other Health Impairment" category or Section 504, according to IDEA regulations (§34 CRF 300.7), in addition to the regulations for public education in our state.

I look forward to your response and to collaborating with you and your staff so that we may ensure a successful educational experience for my child.

Sincerely,

Name   _____

Address   _____

_____

_____

Phone Number _____

Conclusion

THIS book has been designed as a workbook for a very important reason. The collection of worksheets, forms, checklists, charts, websites, and other tools included as reproducible pages provides practical, daily support materials and the guidance necessary to assist teachers and parents as they empower students to become successful learners.

Understanding the importance of attention and behavioral self-regulation and their impact on everyday living is essential to providing the most effective and comprehensive set of strategies, treatments, services, and programs for those individuals with ADHD.

We invite you to use the information, tools, strategies, and resources provided here as you work with those students who have ADHD. The contents of this book also may act as a springboard for further research and the collection of your own successful practices when working in your classrooms and at home as you continue to make a difference in a child's life. The companion title to this book, *School Success for Kids With ADHD*, also will be helpful as a further reference.

References

American Educational Research Association, American Psychological Association, & National Council on Measurement in Education. (1999). *The standards for educational and psychological testing.* Washington, DC: Authors.

American Psychiatric Association. (2000). *Diagnostic and statistical manual of mental disorders* (4th ed., Text rev.). Washington, DC: Author.

Barkley, R. A. (2006). *Attention deficit hyperactivity disorder: A handbook for diagnosis and treatment* (3rd ed.). New York, NY: Guilford.

Barton, J. M., & Starnes, T. T. (1989). Identifying distinguishing characteristics of gifted and talented/learning disabled students. *Roeper Review, 12,* 23–29.

Baum, S. (1990). *Gifted but learning disabled: A puzzling paradox.* Reston, VA: Council for Exceptional Children. (ERIC Document Reproduction Service No. ED321484)

Biederman, J., Farone, S., Milberger, S., Guite, J., Mick, E., Chen, L., . . . Perrin, J. (1996). A prospective 4-year follow-up of attention-deficit hyperactivity and related disorders. *Archives of General Psychiatry, 53,* 437–446.

Cline, S., & Schwartz, D. (1999) *Diverse populations of gifted children.* Englewood Cliffs, NJ: Merrill/Prentice Hall.

Council for Exceptional Children. (2000). *Making assessment accommodations: A toolkit for educators.* Reston, VA: Author.

Dendy, C. A. Z. (2000). *Teaching teens with ADD and ADHD: A quick reference guide for teachers and parents.* Bethesda, MD: Woodbine House.

Dendy, C. A. Z. (Ed.). (2006). *CHADD educator's manual on attention deficit/hyperactivity disorder (AD/HD): An in-depth look from an educational perspective.* Landover, MD: CHADD.

Dendy, C. A. Z., & Zeigler, A. (2003). *A bird's eye view of life with ADD and ADHD.* Cedar Bluff, AL: Cherish the Children.

Desikachar, T. K. V. (1995). *The heart of yoga: Developing a personal practice.* Rochester, VT: Inner Traditions International.

DuPaul, G. J., & Eckert, T. L. (1998). Academic interventions for students with attention-deficit/hyperactivity disorder: A review of the literature. *Reading and Writing Quarterly: Overcoming Learning Disabilities, 14,* 59–82.

DuPaul, G. J., & Stoner, G. (2002). Interventions for attention problems. In M. Shinn, H. M. Walker, & G. Stoner (Eds.), *Interventions for academic and behavioral problems II: Preventive and remedial approaches* (pp. 913–938). Bethesda, MD: National Association of School Psychologists.

Fuchs, L. S., Fuchs, D., Eaton, S. B., Hamlett, C., & Karns, K. (2000). Supplementing teacher judgments of mathematics test accommodations with objective data sources. *School Psychology Review, 29,* 65–85.

Gardner, H. (1983). *Frames of mind: The theory of multiple intelligences.* New York, NY: Basic Books.

Harman, P. (Ed.). (2001). *The CHADD information and resource guide to AD/HD.* Landover, MD: CHADD.

Heacox, D. (1991). *Up from under-achievement: How teachers, students, and parents can work together to promote student success.* Minneapolis, MN: Free Spirit Publishing

Hecker, L., Burns, L., Katz, L., Elkind, J., & Elkind, K. (2002). Benefits of assistive reading software for students with attention disorders. *Annals of Dyslexia, 52,* 243–273.

Herrerias, C. T., Perrin, J. M., & Stein, M. T. (2001). The child with ADHD: Using the AAP clinical practice guideline. *American Family Physician, 63,* 1803–1810.

Individuals with Disabilities Education Act, PL 105-17, 111 Stat. 37 (1997).

Individuals with Disabilities Education Improvement Act, PL 108-446, 118 Stat. 2647 (2004).

Kurzweil Educational Systems. (2006). *Kurzweil 3000—Solutions for struggling readers.* Retrieved from http://www.kurzweiledu.com/kurz3000.aspx

Lenz, K., & Schumaker, J. (1999). *Adapting language arts, social studies, and science materials for the inclusive classroom: Volume 3: Grades six through eight.* Reston, VA: Council for Exceptional Children.

Maryland State Department of Education. (1999). *Maryland state performance assessment program.* Baltimore, MD: Author.

Maryland State Department of Education. (2000). *Requirements for accommodating, excusing, and exempting students in Maryland assessment programs.* Baltimore, MD: Author.

Matlen, T. (2008). *Howie Mandel raises awareness about ADHD in adults.* Retrieved from http://www.healthcentral.com/adhd/c/57718/45566/awareness-campaign

Menhard, F. R. (2007). *The facts about Ritalin.* New York, NY: Marshall Cavendish Benchmark.

McIntyre, T. (2004). *Strategies for teaching youth with ADD and ADHD.* Retrieved from http://www.ldonline.org/article/13701

Montgomery County Public Schools. (1983). *Blueprint for study strategies.* Rockville, MD: Author.

Montgomery County Public Schools. (1998). *Checklist for effective instruction of all learners.* Rockville, MD: Author.

Naglieri, J. A. (1999). *Essentials of CAS assessment.* New York, NY: Wiley.

National Association for Gifted Children. (1998). *Students with concomitant gifts and learning disabilities.* Washington, DC: Author.

National Institute of Mental Health. (2008a). *Diagnosis.* Retrieved from http://www.nimh.nih.gov/health/publications/adhd/diagnosis.html

National Institute of Mental Health. (2008b). *Disorders that sometimes accompany ADHD.* Retrieved from http://www.nimh.nih.gov/health/publications/adhd/disorders-that-sometimes-accompany-adhd.shtml

Renzulli, J. S. (1977). *The enrichment triad model: A guide for developing defensible programs for the gifted and talented.* Mansfield Center, CT: Creative Learning Press.

Ricci, M. C., Barnes-Robinson, L., & Jeweler, S. (2006). Helping your children build on their visual-spatial strength in a world of words. *Parenting for High Potential,* 5–7, 30.

Robin, A. L. (n.d.). *Helping your adolescent with ADHD get homework done.* Retrieved from http://www.add.org/articles/teenhomework.html

Section 504 of the Rehabilitation Act, 29 U.S.C. Section 706 et. Seq. (1973).

Silverman, S. M., Iseman, J. S., & Jeweler, S. (2009). *School success for kids with ADHD.* Waco, TX: Prufrock Press.

Thurlow, M., House, A., Scott, D., & Ysseldyke, J. (2001) *State participation and accommodation policies for students with disabilities.* Minneapolis, MN: National Center for Educational Outcomes.

Tomlinson, C. A. (1999). *The differentiated classroom: Responding to the needs of all learners.* Alexandria, VA: Association for Supervision and Curriculum Development.

U.S. Department of Education. (2004). *Teaching children with attention deficit hyperactivity disorder: Instructional strategies and practices.* Retrieved from http://www.ldonline.org/article/8797

Weinfeld, R., Barnes-Robinson, L., Jeweler, S., & Roffman Shevitz, B. (2006). *Smart kids with learning difficulties: Overcoming obstacles and realizing potential.* Waco, TX: Prufrock Press.

Authors' Note

The following tools were reprinted with permission from *Smart Kids With Learning Difficulties: Overcoming Obstacles and Realizing Potential* (Weinfeld et al., 2006): 34–53, 55–56, 78, 82, 84, 92.

The following tools were reprinted with permission from *School Success for Kids With ADHD* (Silverman et al., 2009): 80, 85, 89, 96.

Tool 97 was contributed to this volume by Shoshana Silverman Belisle.

About the Authors

Jacqueline S. Iseman, Ph.D., is a licensed psychologist with a private practice in Potomac, MD. She received her bachelor's degree from Cornell University, and her Ph.D. in clinical psychology from George Mason University. She has worked in a variety of hospital, school, and clinic settings including Children's National Medical Center in Washington, DC, the Devereux Foundation's Day School in Pennsylvania, and several private practices in Maryland and Virginia. Iseman's research on differential diagnosis of ADHD was published in the article "Performance of Children with Attention Deficit Hyperactivity Disorder and Anxiety/Depression on the WISC-III and Cognitive Assessment System (CAS)." In Iseman's private practice, Hands on Health Psychological Services, LLC (http://www.handsonpsychology.com), she provides support and guidance to her clients in order to provide pathways toward developing healthier and more fulfilling lives. Her areas of expertise include working with children, adolescents, and families providing psychotherapy, consultations, and assessment. Iseman enjoys treating clients with a broad range of psychological concerns. Her approach is practical and comprehensive, addressing each individual's issues within the context of the family, school, and community.

Stephan M. Silverman, Ph.D., retired in July 2008 after 30 years as a school psychologist in the Montgomery County Public Schools (MCPS) in Montgomery County, MD. He has maintained a private practice since 1975. Silverman specializes in the diagnosis, treatment, and instruction of children, adolescents, and adults with attention deficits, learning disabilities, and low incidence developmental disorders, including autistic spectrum disorders. He specializes in working with parents of children with disabilities and children who underachieve and evaluates and counsels young adults with disabilities in life transitions. He has lectured nationally to a wide group of psychologists, educators, and related health providers on topics such as learning disabilities, ADHD, and Asperger's syndrome. Silverman worked in a private research group investigating combat stress in American helicopter pilots during the Vietnam conflict. He also served as a child psychologist in a developmental assessment clinic in Israel in the early 1970s. Silverman is the coauthor of the best-selling *School Success for Kids With Asperger's Syndrome* with Rich Weinfeld, also published by Prufrock Press.

Sue Jeweler, a retired teacher, spent her 30-year career in Maryland's Montgomery County Public Schools. Jeweler has been a consultant to the John F. Kennedy Center for the Performing Arts, the Smithsonian Institution, National Geographic, Berns & Kay, and Street Law. Her expertise has been used in a variety of projects with an outreach to teachers nationally and internationally. She has coauthored two educational kits, numerous journal articles, and more than 40 books including the best-selling *Smart Kids With Learning Difficulties: Overcoming Obstacles and Realizing Potential*. Jeweler, an award-winning educator, is the recipient of the prestigious *Washington Post* Agnes Meyer Outstanding Teaching Award. She is listed in *Who's Who Among America's Teachers*, *Who's Who of American Women*, and the *International Who's Who*. She coestablished Creative Family Projects, LLC, which identifies problems and provides solutions by synthesizing information from organizations, institutions, and corporations into booklets and training modules for the benefit of children, youth, and families. Jeweler is married with children and has one grandchild.